Query Answer Authentication

Synthesis Lectures on Data Management

Editor
M. Tamer Özsu, *University of Waterloo*

Synthesis Lectures on Data Management is edited by Tamer Özsu of the University of Waterloo. The series will publish 50- to 125 page publications on topics pertaining to data management. The scope will largely follow the purview of premier information and computer science conferences, such as ACM SIGMOD, VLDB, ICDE, PODS, ICDT, and ACM KDD. Potential topics include, but not are limited to: query languages, database system architectures, transaction management, data warehousing, XML and databases, data stream systems, wide scale data distribution, multimedia data management, data mining, and related subjects.

Query Answer Authentication
HweeHwa Pang and Kian-Lee Tan
2012

Declarative Networking
Boon Thau Loo and Wenchao Zhou
2012

Full-Text (Substring) Indexes in External Memory
Marina Barsky, Ulrike Stege, and Alex Thomo
2011

Spatial Data Management
Nikos Mamoulis
2011

Database Repairing and Consistent Query Answering
Leopoldo Bertossi
2011

Managing Event Information: Modeling, Retrieval, and Applications
Amarnath Gupta and Ramesh Jain
2011

© Springer Nature Switzerland AG 2022

Reprint of original edition © Morgan & Claypool 2012

Query Answer Authentication

HweeHwa Pang and Kian-Lee Tan

ISBN: 978-3-031-00759-0   paperback
ISBN: 978-3-031-01887-9   ebook

DOI 10.1007/978-3-031-01887-9

A Publication in the Springer series
SYNTHESIS LECTURES ON DATA MANAGEMENT

Lecture #24
Series Editor: M. Tamer Özsu, *University of Waterloo*
Series ISSN
Synthesis Lectures on Data Management
Print 2153-5418   Electronic 2153-5426

Query Answer Authentication

HweeHwa Pang
Singapore Management University

Kian-Lee Tan
National University of Singapore

SYNTHESIS LECTURES ON DATA MANAGEMENT #24

ABSTRACT

In data publishing, the owner delegates the role of satisfying user queries to a third-party publisher. As the servers of the publisher may be untrusted or susceptible to attacks, we cannot assume that they would always process queries correctly, hence there is a need for users to authenticate their query answers.

This book introduces various notions that the research community has studied for defining the correctness of a query answer. In particular, it is important to guarantee the completeness, authenticity and minimality of the answer, as well as its freshness. We present authentication mechanisms for a wide variety of queries in the context of relational and spatial databases, text retrieval, and data streams. We also explain the cryptographic protocols from which the authentication mechanisms derive their security properties.

KEYWORDS

correctness of query answer, data integrity, database security, outsourced database

Contents

Preface

In the data publishing model, also known as database-as-a-service, a data owner outsources the database management functionalities to a third-party publisher. Users who need to access the database of the owner will then submit their queries to the publisher. The model is gaining popularity commercially as it reduces the total cost of ownership (in terms of manpower, hardware and software costs) to the data owner and offers quality service to the consumers of the data.

As the publisher may be malicious or its systems may be vulnerable to security breaches, one key challenge in data publishing is to ensure query answer authenticity: Given that the publisher may not be trusted, it is critical for end users to have an assurance that the query answers returned by the publisher are indeed the same answers that the owner would have given. This book brings together a collection of authentication mechanisms that have been investigated for various application domains to address the challenge.

In Chapter 1, we begin by introducing the data publishing model. We discuss its benefits, and formulate the associated system and threat models. We then bring out the need for users to check the authenticity of their query answers, and summarize the cost factors to take into account in developing a query authentication mechanism.

In Chapter 2, we lay the foundation and background knowledge for the rest of the book. In particular, we review cryptographic protocols that form the building blocks for the query answer authentication schemes that follow. We also examine the costs of various cryptographic primitives.

Chapter 3 presents query authentication schemes for relational databases. We identify the key requirements of an effective authentication scheme. We examine schemes built upon both Merkle Hash Tree and signature aggregation for a wide variety of relational queries, including selection, projection, join as well as aggregation. We also look at incorporating authentication information into index structures in order to facilitate efficient processing.

In Chapter 4, we focus on authentication mechanisms for spatial databases. In particular, we present authentication methods for window, range, kNN and RNN queries. These methods are based on Merkle Hash Tree, signature chain as well as geometry, and employ spatial data structures like R-tree and KD-tree.

Unlike traditional relational and spatial databases, text search offers a different set of challenges.

Even if the search engine returns all the relevant documents, it may alter their ranking within the result. In Chapter 5, we investigate methods for guaranteeing the correctness of query answers for text search. These methods require pre-certification of the inverted lists that store the frequency of every combination of document and term, from which document scores are computed. Adaptations of the threshold algorithm to support query answer authentication are presented.

In Chapter 6, we describe techniques for authenticating streaming data. Here, authentication mechanisms must additionally ensure that the relative order of each datum is preserved. We present methods based on Merkle Hash Tree for sliding window queries as well as aggregation sliding window queries.

Finally, Chapter 7 concludes the book. Query answer authentication is a relatively young field that is becoming increasingly important. There are many outstanding challenges and issues that merit further research before the field matures. We highlight some of the more interesting ones in this chapter.

This book can be used as a reference for a variety of audience. It can serve as a reference text in graduate level database security courses that cover query authentication. It also provides a good survey to graduate students working on securing databases under the database-as-a-service model (e.g., database outsourcing and cloud computing). Researchers, technologists and developers will also find this book a good source for learning more about assuring users of the authenticity of their query answers

HweeHwa Pang and Kian-Lee Tan
February 2012

Acknowledgments

We are thankful to several people who have made this book possible. In particular, M. Tamer Özsu, Editor of the Synthesis Lectures on Data Management, offered us the opportunity to write this book. Tamer also read an earlier draft of the book and provided valuable comments that improve its literary style. Throughout this project, Diane D. Cerra, the Executive Editor of Morgan & Claypool, provided us with excellent editorial support necessary for the completion of this book.

HweeHwa Pang and Kian-Lee Tan
February 2012

CHAPTER 1

Introduction

In data publishing, a data owner delegates the role of satisfying user queries to a third-party publisher [Devanbu et al., 2000, Miklau and Suciu, 2003]. This model is applicable to a wide range of computing platforms, including database caching [Luo et al., 2002], content delivery network [Saroiu et al., 2002], edge computing [Margulius, 2002], database outsourcing [Hacigumus et al., 2002], P2P databases [Huebsch et al., 2003], etc.

The data publishing model offers a number of advantages over conventional client-server architecture where the owner also undertakes the processing of user queries. By pushing application logic and data processing from the owner out to multiple publisher servers situated near user clusters, network latency can be reduced. Adding publisher servers is also likely to be a cheaper way to achieve scalability than fortifying the owner's data center and provisioning more network bandwidth for every user. Finally, the data publishing model removes the single point of failure in the owner's data center, hence reducing the database's susceptibility to denial of service attacks and improving service availability.

To illustrate, a financial information provider could push historical stock prices, together with analytics software, to proxy servers operated by partner ISPs (Internet Service Provider). Such an arrangement enables users to run different pricing and risk models off the proxy servers directly instead of depending on a central data center that might be situated thousands of miles away, thus reducing communication latency and processing bottlenecks.

While there are many advantages, publishing data through third-party servers also raises security concerns. The number of successful attacks on online servers has grown tremendously over the last decade. The types of attacks range from tampering of data, to unauthorized access of sensitive information like credit card numbers and user passwords. The targets of the attacks include government, large corporations, and even e-business sites that we would expect to have been professionally administered and secured. This shows that it is very difficult to guarantee the security of online servers over extended periods of time, especially where the servers are beyond the administrative domain of the data owner.

In this book, we study methods for users to authenticate their query answers, in other words to check their "correctness", in the context of the data publishing model. The general solution approach stems from the observation that, in many organizations, data are created and maintained on a content management platform like Interwoven, before being deployed onto (public-facing) query servers. This architecture, as depicted in Figure 1.1, can be exploited to improve system security as follows: The content manager can reside in a closed, secure network (the "Owner") to ensure the integrity of the master database. In addition, authentication information is built into the database, before it is deployed onto one or more query servers (the "third-party server"). From the authentication information, the server is able to create for each query answer a correctness proof. If any server gets compromised and returns a wrong query answer, the user would detect a mismatch with the accompanying correctness proof and be alerted.

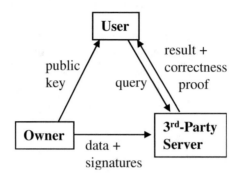

Figure 1.1: System Model.

1.1   SYSTEM AND THREAT MODELS

We now elaborate on the system model in Figure 1.1, which supports three distinct roles:

- The data owner maintains a master database, and distributes it with one or more associated signatures that proves the authenticity of the database. Any data item that has a matching signature is accepted by the user to be trustworthy.

- The server hosts the database, and performs query processing on behalf of the owner, possibly after some query-rewriting to comply with the access control rules on the database. The access control model may be discretionary, mandatory or role-based (e.g., see [Sandhu and Samarati, 1994]). Regardless of the exact model, the server should ensure that only data that satisfy the rewritten queries are returned, so as to avoid contradicting the access control rules. There could be several servers that are situated at the edge of the network, near the user applications. The server is not required to be trusted, so the query answers that it generates must be accompanied by some "correctness proof", in the form of a *verification object* (VO) derived from the database and signatures issued by the owner.

- The user issues queries to the server explicitly, or else gets redirected to the server, e.g., by the owner or a directory service. To verify the query answers, the user obtains the public key of the owner through an authenticated channel, such as a public key certificate issued by a certificate authority.

There are several potential security considerations in the above system model. Given that the servers are not trusted, one concern is privacy of the data. Obviously, an adversary who gains access to the operating system or hardware of a server may be able to browse through the database, or make illegal copies of the data. Solutions to mitigate this concern include encryption (e.g., MSEFS[1], E4M[2], PGPdisk[3]) and steganographic storage (e.g., [Anderson et al., 1998, Pang et al., 2003], DriveCrypt[4]), and are orthogonal to our work here.

Another concern relates to user authentication and access control, in specifying what actions each user is permitted to perform. Those issues have been studied extensively (e.g., [Chokani, 1992, Neuman and Ts'o, 1994, Sandhu and Samarati, 1994]) and are complementary to this work.

Our primary concern addressed in this book is the threat that a dishonest server may return incorrect query answers to the users, whether intentionally or under the influence of an adversary. An adversary who is cognizant of the data organization in the publisher server may attempt to make logical alterations to the data, thus inducing incorrect query results.

1.2 COST FACTORS

Assuming we have an authentication scheme that is well designed and provides satisfactory correctness proof for query answers, we would be concerned about the costs imposed during data preparation, query evaluation, and update processing. As identified by Li et al. [2006], the cost factors relating to the system model in Figure 1.1 include the following:

- the computation cost incurred by the owner in generating the authentication information and digital signature(s) for the database;

- the communication cost for transmitting the authentication information and signature(s) from the owner to the third-party server;

- the storage cost at the server for the authentication information and signature(s);

- the computation cost incurred by the server in generating the VO for a query answer;

- the communication cost for transmitting the VO from the server to the user; and

- the computation cost that the user client expends to verify the query answer against the VO.

Whereas in conventional query processing the computation overhead can often be ignored because it is dominated by I/O costs, query answer authentication schemes derive their security properties from cryptographic constructs that could be computationally demanding. It is therefore necessary to systematically assess the practicality of an authentication scheme against all the cost factors.

---

[1] http://technet.microsoft.com/en-us/library/cc700811.aspx; last accessed January 2012
[2] http://members.multimania.co.uk/e4m; last accessed January 2012
[3] http://www.pgpi.org/products/pgpdisk/; last accessed January 2012
[4] http://www.securstar.com/disk_encryption.php; last accessed January 2012

1.3   ORGANIZATION

In Chapter 2, we set the foundation by reviewing the cryptographic protocols that form the building blocks for the query answer authentication schemes. Following that, Chapters 3, 4, 5, and 6 introduce authentication schemes for relational queries, spatial queries, text search queries, and queries over data streams, respectively. Finally, Chapter 7 concludes the book, and discusses outstanding challenges that require further research.

CHAPTER 2

Cryptography Foundation

The query authentication schemes that we cover in this book make extensive use of cryptographic constructs. In this chapter, we give a working definition of those constructs; the reader is encouraged to refer to the original articles for details. We also provide recent timing measurements for the key constructs, to give the reader a sense of their relative costs.

2.1 CRYPTOGRAPHIC PROTOCOLS

One-Way Hash: A one-way hash function, denoted as $\mathcal{H}(.)$, works in one direction; it is easy to compute the value $\mathcal{H}(m)$ for a given message $m \in \{0, 1\}^*$, but computationally infeasible to find a message m that hashes to a given $\mathcal{H}(.)$ value. We refer to $\mathcal{H}(m)$ as the hash or digest of m. A common hash function is SHA [SHA, 2001] with 160-bit digests. Over time, longer digests are expected to be used to compensate for the increasing computational power of the adversaries.

Cryptographic Signature: A cryptographic signature protocol is a tool for verifying the origin, authenticity and integrity of signed messages. The protocol involves a pair of public and private keys. Only the holder of the private key can use it to generate cryptographic signatures on messages. The corresponding public key is distributed openly, for anyone to verify a message against its signature. RSA [Rivest et al., 1978] and ECC [Boneh et al., 2003] are two standard signature algorithms. We refer to a cryptographic signature simply as signature.

Cryptographic Accumulator: First proposed by Benaloh and de Mare [1993], the one-way accumulator is a method for collectively authenticating a set of elements so that membership of any element can be tested. One of the common accumulators defines the cumulative value for n elements $d_1, d_2, \ldots, d_n$ to be $C = a^{\prod_{i=1}^{n} d_i} \mod N$. In this formulation, N is chosen as the product of two large prime numbers, and a is co-prime with N. The membership of any element d_i can be proved by returning the proof $C^- = a^{\prod_{j \neq i} d_j} \mod N$ to the user, who will then verify that $(C^-)^{d_i} \mod N = C$. For any element that is not a legitimate member of the collection, it would be computationally infeasible for an adversary to devise a matching proof.

As the proof generation involves modulo exponentiation, it would be very expensive to derive C^- from scratch for individual queries at runtime. To avoid that, Goodrich et al. [2002] proposed constructing a binary tree over the elements, in which each node accumulates all the elements outside of the subtree under that node. The leaves of the tree provide the proof for every element so a membership test can be satisfied in constant time, at the expense of linear space and update overheads.

Merkle Hash Tree (MHT): The Merkle Hash Tree is a method for collectively authenticating a set of messages [Merkle, 1989]. Consider the example in Figure 2.1, where the owner of messages m_1, m_2, m_3, m_4 wishes to authenticate them. The MHT is built bottom-up, by first computing the leaf nodes N_i as the digests $\mathcal{H}(m_i)$ of the messages, where $\mathcal{H}(.)$ is a one-way hash function. The value of each internal node is derived from its two child nodes, e.g., $N_{1,2} = \mathcal{H}(N_1|N_2)$, where | denotes concatenation. Finally, the digest $N_{1,2,3,4}$ of the root node is signed. The tree can be used to authenticate any subset of the data values, in conjunction with a verification object (VO). For example, to authenticate m_1, the VO contains N_2, $N_{3,4}$ and the signed root $N_{1,2,3,4}$. Upon receipt of m_1, any addressee may verify its authenticity by first computing $\mathcal{H}(m_1)$ and then checking whether $\mathcal{H}(\mathcal{H}(\mathcal{H}(m_1)|N_2)|N_{3,4})$ matches the signed root $N_{1,2,3,4}$. If so, m_1 is accepted; otherwise, m_1, N_2, $N_{3,4}$ and/or the signed root have been tampered with. The MHT is a binary tree, although it can be extended to multiway trees and directed acyclic graphs [Martel et al., 2004].

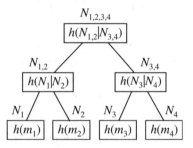

Figure 2.1: Example of a Merkle Hash Tree.

RSA Signature Aggregation: The RSA algorithm [Rivest et al., 1978] works as follows. Let p and q be distinct large prime numbers of similar length, $N = pq$, and $\phi(N) = (p-1)(q-1)$ be the Euler's totient. The public key e and private key d are chosen to satisfy the condition $ed = 1 \mod \phi(N)$. Let $\mathcal{H}(.)$ be a one-way hash function. A message $m \in \{0, 1\}^*$ is signed as $\sigma = \mathcal{H}(m)^d \mod N$, and subsequently verified by checking that $\mathcal{H}(m) = \sigma^e \mod N$. Given n messages m_i's with corresponding signatures σ_i's, the aggregate signature $\sigma = \prod_{i=1}^{n} \sigma_i$ can be computed by any (untrusted) party, then used to verify the messages collectively, by checking the equality $\prod_{i=1}^{n} \mathcal{H}(m_i) = \sigma^e \mod N$.

Elliptic Curve Cryptography (ECC): The mathematical operations of ECC are defined over the elliptic curve $y^2 = x^3 + ax + \beta$, where $4a^3 + 2\beta^2 \neq 0$. Each combination of a and β produces a different elliptic curve. All points (x, y) that satisfy the above equation lie on the elliptic curve.

The elliptic curve over a finite operator group G_p [Aschbacher, 2000] is specified by the tuple $\langle p, a, \beta, g, n \rangle$, where:

- p is the order of (i.e., the number of elements in) G_p. SEC [Certicom, 2000] specifies p to be a prime with 112–521 bits;

- a and β define the elliptic curve $y^2 \mod p = x^3 + ax + \beta \mod p$;

- $g = (g_x, g_y)$ is a point on the chosen elliptic curve and a generator for G_p; and

- n is the order of (i.e., the number of points on) the elliptic curve.

The above specification is known to all parties who participate in the ECC protocol. Joux and Nguyen [2003] provided some examples of suitable elliptic curves.

Bilinear Groups: Let G be a multiplicative group[1] of prime order p with generator g. A **Bilinear Map** is a mapping $e : G \times G \to G_T$, where G_T is another multiplicative group of prime order p, that exhibits the following properties:

- bilinear: $\forall u, v \in G$ and $a, b \in \mathbb{Z}, e(au, bv) = e(u, v)^{ab}$;

- computability: $\forall u, v \in G, e(u, v)$ can be computed efficiently; and

- non-degenerate: $e(g, g) \neq 1$.

A bilinear group is a group that has a bilinear map, and on which the **Computational Diffie-Hellman** (CDH) problem is hard. The CDH problem is to compute $h^a \in G$ for given $g, g^a, h \in G$.

Bilinear Aggregate Signature (BAS): Proposed by Boneh et al. [2001, 2003], this is a scheme that enables any set of message-signature pairs $\langle m_i, \sigma_i \rangle$ to be combined in arbitrary order into a single signature for all the messages concerned.

Let G_p be a bilinear group, and $H : G \times \{0, 1\}^* \to G$ be a hash function that maps an element of G together with a binary string to another element in G. The scheme works as follows.

- Key Generation: For each data owner, pick a random private key $x \in \mathbb{Z}_p$. The corresponding public key is $v = x \cdot g, v \in G$.

- Signing: The owner of public key v and private key x can generate a signature σ for message $m \in \{0, 1\}^*$ by computing $h = H(v, m)$ where $h \in G$, followed by $\sigma = x \cdot h$.

- Signature Verification: A message m with signature σ issued by a user with public key v can be verified by computing $h = H(v, m)$, then checking that $e(\sigma, g) = e(h, v)$ holds.

- Aggregation: Given n messages m_i's with accompanying signatures σ_i's issued by one or more signers, any (untrusted) party may derive the aggregate signature as $\sigma = \prod_{i=1}^{n} \sigma_i$, where $\sigma \in G$.

- Aggregate Verification: Given an aggregate signature σ over n messages m_i's that are signed by users with public keys v_i's, the messages can be verified by computing $h_i = H(v_i, m_i)$ for $1 \leq i \leq n$, then checking that the equality $e(\sigma, g) = \prod_{i=1}^{n} e(h_i, v_i)$ holds.

Since σ can be uniquely defined with just its x-coordinate, only that needs to be transmitted for verification purposes.

---

[1] A multiplicative group is an algebraic structure in which any two elements can be multiplied to form a third element, while demonstrating the closure, associativity, identity and invertibility properties.

According to Lenstra and Verheul [2001], an ECC signature that is 160 bits long provides comparable security to a 1024-bit RSA [Rivest et al., 1978] signature. Using shorter signatures enables ECC to achieve lower storage overhead. ECC has been adopted as a replacement for RSA public key cryptography by various government agencies in the US, UK, Canada and other NATO countries [National Security Agency, 2009a,b]. In industry, an ECC Interoperability Forum has been created to ensure that ECC products from participating vendors (including Certicom, IBM, Microsoft, RSA, Sun, Verisign, etc.) will integrate seamlessly. As part of the effort to promote widespread use of ECC, Sun Microsystems has donated ECC code to OpenSSL and the Network Security Services (NSS) library; this brings ECC to the Apache web server and Mozilla browsers, and potentially many other products.

Bloom Filter: A Bloom filter [Bloom, 1970] supports membership checks on a set of b key values R = $\{r_1, r_2, \ldots, r_b\}$. To construct a Bloom filter with m bits, we choose k independent hash functions h_1, $h_2, \ldots, h_k$, each with a range of $[1, m]$. For every $r_i \in R$, the filter bits at positions $h_1(r_i), h_2(r_i), \ldots,$ $h_k(r_i)$ are set to 1. To check whether a given r is in R, we examine the bits at $h_1(r), h_2(r), \ldots, h_k(r)$. If any of the bits is 0, r cannot be in R; otherwise, there is a high probability that r is in R. In other words, false positives are possible, but not false negatives. The false positive rate is

$$FP = \left(1 - \left(1 - \frac{1}{m}\right)^{kb}\right)^k \approx \left(1 - e^{-kb/m}\right)^k .$$

(2.1)

Mathematically, FP is minimized at $k = (m \times ln2)/b$, so $FP = 0.6185^k$. Given the value of b and the target FP rate, we can set k and m accordingly.

2.2   COST OF CRYPTOGRAPHIC PROTOCOLS

In Table 2.1 we compare the costs of the basic cryptographic operations in 160-bit BAS. The readings for Year 2006 were reported by Mykletun et al. [2006], using a Pentium 3 800 MHz CPU with 1 GB memory. The measurements for Year 2009 were obtained on a PC equipped with Intel Core 2 Quad 3GHz CPU and 3GB memory [Pang et al., 2009]. We observe an impressive speed-up of BAS on the new CPU, with one order of magnitude faster ECC signing and almost 40 times faster BAS verification.

Table 2.1 also presents measurements for an RSA-based implementation of signature aggregation; the results correspond to 1024-bit signatures, offering an equivalent level of security to the 160-bit ECC/BAS scheme. Here, the new timings for signing and verifying signatures have all improved over the old ones, due to the faster modulo multiplications on the newer CPU.

Additionally, Table 2.1 includes hash computation costs for different message sizes (using SHA); this operation is important to all schemes, but especially for MHT-based ones. The results show that signature aggregation through condensed RSA or BAS is now viable in terms of computation time. Between the two, RSA is faster while BAS has the advantage of shorter signature length, which translates to lower space requirements.

Table 2.1: Costs of Cryptographic Primitives.		
Operation	**Year 2006**	**Year 2009**
Bilinear Aggregate Signature		
(a) Individual signature		
• Signing	12.0 ms	1.5 ms
• Verification	77.4 ms	40.22 ms
(b) 1000-signature aggregate		
• Aggregation	N.A.	9.06 ms
• Verification	12085.4 ms	331.349 ms
RSA Signature Aggregation		
(a) Individual signature		
• Signing	6.82 ms	6.06 ms
• Verification	0.16 ms	0.087 ms
(b) 1000-signature aggregate		
• Aggregation	N.A.	0.078 ms
• Verification	44.12 ms	0.094 ms
Secure Hashing Algorithm (SHA)		
• 256-byte message	–	1.35 μs
• 512-byte message	–	2.28 μs
• 1024-byte message	–	4.2 μs

CHAPTER 3

Relational Queries

As we saw in Chapter 2, the cryptographic protocols that form the foundation of query answer authentication, particularly the Merkle Hash Tree, are designed for verifying ordered lists. Since a tree-structured index like B^+-tree orders the records in a relation by a designated search key, the applicability of the cryptographic protocols to queries that execute over a tree-structured index is obvious. For this reason, we begin by studying query answer authentication in the context of relational databases.

3.1 BACKGROUND

Emp:

ID	Name	Salary	Dept	Photo	...
005	A	2000	1	...	
002	C	3500	2	...	
001	D	8010	1	...	
004	B	12100	3	...	
003	E	25000	2	...	

Query: SELECT * FROM Emp WHERE Salary < 10000

Figure 3.1: Example database.

As the server cannot be assumed to be a trusted party, a user who submits a query on the database would want certain correctness guarantees for the answer. We illustrate the guarantees with the example in Figure 3.1.

- *Authenticity*: A query answer is authentic if all the values in the answer originated from the data owner. For example, for the **Emp** table and query in Figure 3.1, the server indeed returns the answer { [005, A, 2000, ..], [002, C, 3500, ..], [001, D, 8010, ..] }, and not { [005, C, 2000, ..], [002, A, 3500, ..], [001, D, 8010, ..] } (the names in the first two records have been swapped), nor { [005, A, 2000, ..], [002, C, 3500, ..], [001, D, 8010, ..], [009, X, 8050, ..] } (the last record is spurious).

- *Completeness*: A query answer is complete if every record satisfying the conditions of the user query is included in the answer. For example, the answer { [005, A, 2000, ..], [001, D, 8010, ..] } for the query in Figure 3.1 is incomplete as [002, C, 3500, ..] is omitted.

- *Freshness*: Over time, the data owner may update and re-certify the database. A query answer is fresh, or current, if it is derived from the latest database instance. This implies that the user must be able to detect a query answer that is supported by an old signature.

The verification objects (VO) that provide the above guarantees should satisfy the following requirements.

- *Minimality*: Only records and attribute values that satisfy the conditions of each query are returned. One important motivation for minimality is to avoid contravening any access control rules on the database, which would become (part of) the query conditions through query rewriting.

- *Security*: It is computationally infeasible for a server to cheat by generating a valid VO for an incorrect query answer.

- *Efficiency*: The procedure for the server to generate the VO for a correct (i.e., authentic, complete and fresh) query answer has polynomial complexity. Likewise, the procedure performed by the user to verify a query answer has polynomial complexity.

3.2   SELECTION QUERY

Consider a relation $\mathbf{R}$ with schema $\langle K, A_1, A_2, .., A_m \rangle$. $\mathbf{R}$ contains n records $[r_1, r_2, .., r_n]$, sorted on K. The **range selection** operation $\sigma_{K \in [\alpha, \beta]}$ on $\mathbf{R}$ produces the answer $\sigma_{K \in [\alpha, \beta]}(\mathbf{R}) = \{r \mid r \in \mathbf{R} \text{ and } \alpha \leq r.K \leq \beta\}$.

To enable the server to prove that $\sigma_{K \in [\alpha, \beta]}(\mathbf{R})$ is correct, the data owner certifies the sorted relation. The answer should be a sequence of records $[r_l, r_{l+1}, \ldots, r_u]$, $1 \leq l \leq u \leq n$, within the sorted $\mathbf{R}$ such that:

(a) the boundaries r_l and r_u are correct, in particular, r_l satisfies $l = 1$ or $r_{l-1}.K < \alpha$, while $u = n$ or $r_{u+1}.K > \beta$ holds for r_u;

(b) the records in the answer run contiguously in the sorted relation.

3.2.1   OVERVIEW OF AUTHENTICATION TECHNIQUES FOR RANGE SELECTION

Most of the existing methods for query answer verification fall under two categories – MHT-based and signature aggregation ones. The MHT-based approaches incorporate an MHT into the data index to facilitate verification (e.g., [Bertino et al., 2004, Devanbu et al., 2003, Pang and Tan,

2004]). Nuckolls [2005] proposed a variation of the MHT that maintains a certified one-way accumulator over the digests of selected nodes; this allows a consolidated evidence to replace the neighboring digests along the path from those nodes to the root, thus reducing the size of the VO. That variation was extended to multiple hash tree levels by Goodrich et al. [2008], who also showed that replay attacks could be eliminated by periodically re-signing the timestamped accumulator. Mouratidis et al. [2009] proposed splitting the authentication structure from the data index to provide architectural flexibility and better performance.

The most representative MHT scheme for disk-resident data is the Embedded Merkle B-tree (EMB$^-$ tree) by Li et al. [2006]. The idea is to index the data with a B$^+$-tree [Comer, 1979], and to embed into it an MHT with the same fan-out. Similar to the original MHT, the root digest is signed by the owner. Posed a range query, the server returns, in addition to the qualifying tuples, two *boundary* ones, p^- and p^+, falling immediately to the left and to the right of the range. The VO contains all the left (right) sibling hashes to the path of p^- (p^+). Upon receipt of the answer, the user calculates the hashes of the returned tuples, and combines them with the VO to reproduce the MHT root digest. If the latter matches the owner's signature, the answer is deemed legitimate.

Signature aggregation schemes [Narasimha and Tsudik, 2006, Pang et al., 2005] require a signature per tuple. With the database ordered on attribute K, the owner hashes and signs every triple of consecutive data tuples. Posed a range selection query on K, the server returns the qualifying data, along with hashes of the first tuple to the left and the first tuple to the right of the range. The signatures of all the result tuples are aggregated and placed into the VO. Finally, the user verifies that the "chained" result tuples and boundary hashes match the aggregate signature. This scheme, initially designed for one-dimensional data, was subsequently extended to multi-dimensional index structures [Cheng and Tan, 2009, Cheng et al., 2006].

A systematic comparison of MHT versus signature aggregation (using condensed RSA) was reported by Li et al. [2006]. The findings there overwhelmingly favored the MHT approach: (a) an RSA signature is typically 1024 bits in length, so signing all the data tuples requires substantially larger space than the MHT, in which each digest occupies just 160 bits; and (b) a hashing operation in the MHT can be performed in roughly 3 μs. In contrast, signature aggregation involves modular multiplication, signing and verification operations that are, respectively, 100, 10,000 and 1,000 times slower than hashing. The only advantage of signature aggregation is its smaller proof and, thus, its lower transmission overhead. A subsequent study by Pang et al. [2009] factored in concurrency control and found that signature aggregation allows concurrent updates to different records, whereas MHT requires each update to lock the signature on the root and precludes concurrent updates.

3.2.2   MERKLE HASH TREE TECHNIQUE

The Merkle Hash Tree (MHT) can be applied directly to check the answer for a range selection query. Suppose that the search key K is defined over the domain $(\mathcal{L}, \mathcal{U}) \subset \mathbb{Z}$. The data owner augments the sorted relation with two fictitious records r_0 and r_{n+1}, such that $r_0.K = \mathcal{L}$ and $r_{n+1}.K = \mathcal{U}$. This changes the sorted relation to $\mathbf{R} = [r_0, r_1, r_2, .., r_n, r_{n+1}]$. Following that, an MHT $\mathcal{T}$, with a digital signature $sign(\mathcal{T})$ at the root, is built on **R**. The MHT is deposited with the server along with **R**. To prove $\sigma_{K \in [\alpha, \beta]}(\mathbf{R}) = [r_l, r_{l+1}, \ldots, r_u]$, the server returns it with an accompanying verification object (VO).

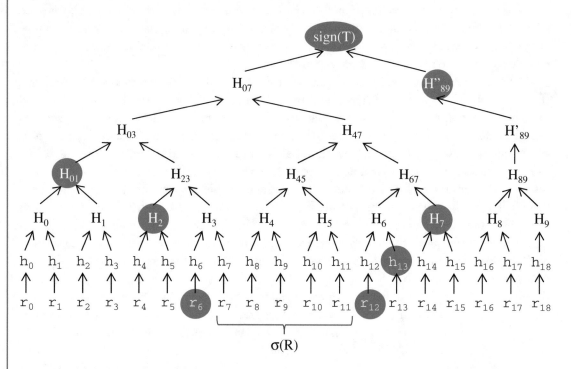

Figure 3.2: Authenticate a selection answer with MHT.

To illustrate, consider the example in Figure 3.2. In the example, an MHT $\mathcal{T}$ is built on the augmented **R** = $[r_0, r_1, \ldots, r_{18}]$, in which r_0 and r_{18} are the two fictitious records added at both ends of the sorted relation. Suppose that a selection query $\sigma(R)$ produces the answer $[r7, \ldots, r_{11}]$. The accompanying VO contains r_6, H_2, H_{01}, r_{12}, h_{13}, H_7, H_{89}'', and the signature $sign(\mathcal{T})$; those items in the VO are printed against a dark circle in the figure. The digest H_{89}'' is returned instead of H_{89}' to avoid revealing to the user that there is only one branch, hence there are no more than 8 records, under H_{89}'. Similarly, returning H_{89} would have disclosed unnecessary information to the user—that there are no more than 4 records under H_{89}''. With the selection answer and the VO, the user can compute the root digest of the MHT, and check whether it matches the signature provided.

In general, for a selection answer $[r_l, \ldots, r_u]$, the VO includes:

- r_{l-1}, together with any left sibling(s) of its ancestors in the MHT; and

- r_{u+1}, together with any right sibling(s) of its ancestors in the MHT.

Here, two nodes are siblings if they share the same parent in the MHT. Algorithm 1 gives the procedure for generating the VO.

Algorithm 1 VO Construction with the MHT for selection answer.

Input: Selection answer $\sigma(R) = [r_l, \ldots, r_u]$, MHT $\mathcal{T}$ with signature $sign(\mathcal{T})$.
Output: Verification object VO.

1: VO = $\{r_{l-1}\}$.
2: N = parent node of r_{l-1} in $\mathcal{T}$.
3: **while** $N \neq sign(\mathcal{T})$ **do**
4:     **if** N has left sibling(s) in $\mathcal{T}$ **then**
5:         Append the left sibling(s) to VO.
6:     **end if**
7:     N = parent node of N.
8: **end while**
9: VO = VO $\cup \{r_{u+1}\}$.
10: N = parent node of r_{u+1} in $\mathcal{T}$.
11: **while** $N \neq sign(\mathcal{T})$ **do**
12:     **if** N has right sibling(s) in $\mathcal{T}$ **then**
13:         Append the right sibling(s) to VO.
14:     **end if**
15:     N = parent node of N.
16: **end while**
17: VO = VO $\cup \{sign(\mathcal{T})\}$.

Denoting the cardinality of the augmented relation $\mathbf{R}$ by $|\mathbf{R}|$, the height of the MHT is $\log_2 |\mathbf{R}|$, meaning that r_{l-1} and r_{u+1} each has $\log_2 |\mathbf{R}|$ ancestors excluding the signature at the root. On average, each ancestor of r_{l-1} (r_{u+1}) has a 50% chance of having a left (right, respectively) sibling. Therefore, the VO is expected to contain $\log_2 |\mathbf{R}|$ node digests altogether, in addition to r_{l-1}, r_{u+1} and $sign(\mathcal{T})$.

The above basic MHT solution has a fan-out of 2, and a tree height of $\log_2 |\mathcal{R}|$. This has two disadvantages. First, for large databases the MHT will need to reside on disk, and fetching each node will incur a random I/O operation. Since the number of MHT nodes needed in the VO is proportional to the tree height, so is the associated I/O cost. Second, the VO has to be transmitted to the user, making the communication cost proportional to the tree height too. For these reasons, it would be more efficient to use a large fan-out.

Continuing the example in Figure 3.2, Figure 3.3 shows an MHT with a fan-out of 8 over the same relation $\mathbf{R}$. Each internal node of the MHT is derived by hashing the concatenation of its child digests. For example, $H_0 = \mathcal{H}(h_0|h_1|\ldots|h_7)$. The node digests that are needed in the VO

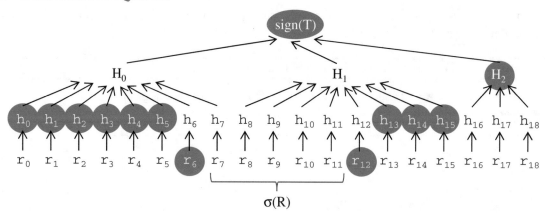

Figure 3.3: A Merkle Hash Tree with a fan-out of f.

accompanying the selection answer $[r_7, \ldots, r_{11}]$ are also printed against dark circles. The current MHT has a height of 2. All the child digests under each node are stored in the same disk page. Thus, h_0 to h_7 are assigned to one page, h_8 to h_{15} to another page, h_{16} to h_{18} to the third page, and the internal nodes H_0 to H_2 to the fourth page. With this storage scheme, we need only 3 I/Os to retrieve the required node digests in the VO for the selection query shown in the figure.

Generalizing, an MHT with a fan-out of f over the augmented relation **R** has a height of $\log_f |\mathbf{R}|$, and each internal node of the MHT is derived by hashing the concatenation of its f child digests. We can still generate the VO for a selection answer $\sigma(\mathbf{R}) = [r_l, \ldots, r_u]$ with Algorithm 1. On average, each ancestor of r_{l-1} has $f/2$ left siblings to be included in the VO, whereas each ancestor of r_{u+1} has $f/2$ right siblings. Thus, the VO is expected to hold $f \log_f |\mathbf{R}|$ node digests altogether, in addition to r_{l-1}, r_{u+1} and $sign(\mathcal{T})$, smaller than the VO obtained with the binary MHT.

To further reduce the size of the VO, Li et al. [2006] proposed to derive each internal node of the MHT through a binary MHT over the f child digests; the result is an Embedded MHT (EMB$^-$). Their technique is illustrated in Figure 3.4, which shows an EMB$^-$ over the same relation **R** and selection query $\sigma(\mathbf{R}) = [r_7, \ldots, r_{11}]$ in our running example. The EMB$^-$ has a height of 2, just like the MHT with fan-out 8. The binary MHT that produces $sign(\mathcal{T})$ from the internal digests H_{03}, H_{47} and H_{89} is embedded in a shaded rectangle, to signify that it is re-computed on-demand and not stored. Likewise, H_{03} is produced by an embedded binary MHT over h_0 to h_7. To generate the node digests in the VO for the example query, the server incurs only 3 I/Os:

- it retrieves the page containing h_0 to h_7, and recomputes H_2 and H_{01} for the VO;

- it retrieves the page containing h_8 to h_{15}, from which h_{13} and H_7 are calculated for the VO; and

- it retrieves the page containing H_{03}, H_{47} and H_{89}, and recomputes H'_{89} for the VO.

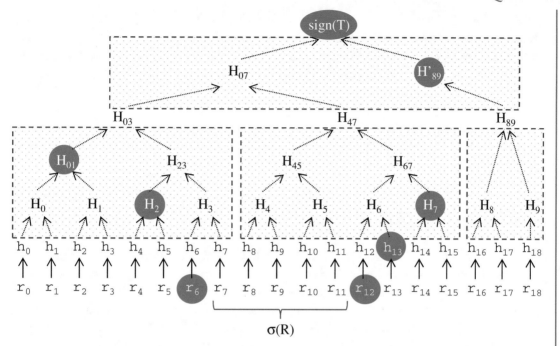

Figure 3.4: Embedded Merkle Hash Tree (EMB⁻).

In general, an EMB⁻ with a fan-out of f over the augmented relation $\mathbf{R}$ has a height of $\log_f |\mathbf{R}|$. For a selection answer $\sigma(\mathbf{R}) = [r_l, \ldots, r_u]$, the left siblings of each ancestor of r_{l-1} are represented by $\log_2 f/2$ digests on the average; likewise, the right siblings of each ancestor of r_{u+1} are represented by $\log_2 f/2$ digests. The VO thus is expected to include $2\log_2 f/2 \cdot \log_f |\mathbf{R}|$ node digests altogether, in addition to r_{l-1}, r_{u+1} and $sign(\mathcal{T})$.

The ability to accommodate an arbitrarily large fan-out f allows the EMB⁻ to be readily incorporated into a B⁺-tree. Specifically, for each internal (leaf) node of the B⁺-tree node, an embedded MHT over the index (data) entries is used to generate the node digest. The digest of a node is stored with the corresponding child pointer in its parent node, so that all the sibling digests for any node can be found with one I/O operation to retrieve its parent. Obviously, storing child digests within the internal nodes has the undesirable effect of reducing the fan-out of the B⁺-tree, increasing its height and hence the I/O cost. This is why Mouratidis et al. [2009] concluded that maintaining separate EMB⁻ and B⁺-tree structures leads to much quicker query processing and VO generation. Additionally, that avoids modifying existing B⁺-tree implementations, which is an important practical consideration.

3.2.3   SIGNATURE AGGREGATION TECHNIQUE

As an alternative to EMB$^-$, we could employ the signature chaining scheme ([Pang and Tan, 2008, Pang et al., 2005]) which is based on signature aggregation. We describe the scheme below, and refer interested readers to the original paper for the security and complexity analyses.

Basic Signature Chaining

In signature chaining, each record has an associated digital signature that is used to verify that the answer for a selection query, $\sigma_{K \in [\alpha, \beta]}(\mathbf{R})$, is complete. The following two conditions together ensure completeness.

- *Contiguity*: Each pair of successive entries in $\sigma_{K \in [\alpha, \beta]}(\mathbf{R})$ also appear consecutively in $\mathbf{R}$. This can be checked by making the signature of each record in $\mathbf{R}$ dependent on the key value of its immediate left and right neighbors.

- *Correct boundaries*: r_a and r_b are the first and last records, respectively, in $\mathbf{R}$ that satisfy the query condition. Conceptually, the signature of r_a is constructed to be dependent on $\mathcal{H}(r_a.K - r_{a-1}.K)$ where $\mathcal{H}$ is an additive hash function such that $\mathcal{H}(x + y) = \mathcal{H}(x) \circ \mathcal{H}(y)$ for some operator $\circ$. To prove $r_{a-1}.K < \alpha$ without disclosing r_{a-1}, the server returns $\mathcal{H}(\alpha - r_{a-1}.K)$, and the user then combines it with $\mathcal{H}(r_a.K - \alpha)$ to obtain $\mathcal{H}(r_a.K - r_{a-1}.K)$ for matching with the signature. As long as $h(x)$ for $x \leq 0$ is either undefined or computationally infeasible to derive, the server would not be able to cheat by returning a legitimate $\mathcal{H}(\alpha - r_{a-1}.K)$ if in fact $r_{a-1}.K \geq \alpha$. A similar technique enables the verification of $r_{b+1}.K > \beta$.

Furthermore, to check the authenticity of the query answer, the attribute values of each record r_i in $\mathbf{R}$ also contribute to its signature. We begin by detailing a scheme for integer keys, before generalizing it to other attribute types.

1. Preparation

To simplify the solution, the data owner inserts two boundary records r_0 and r_{n+1}, where $r_0.K = \mathcal{L}$ and $r_{n+1}.K = \mathcal{U}$, so the sorted relation becomes $\mathbf{R} = [r_0, r_1, .., r_n, r_{n+1}]$. We assume that $\mathcal{L}$ and $\mathcal{U}$ are known to everyone.

As explained earlier, for checking boundaries $r_{a-1}.K < \alpha$ and $r_{b+1}.K > \beta$, the record signature has to incorporate the output of an additive hash function on the difference between $r_a.K$ and $r_{a-1}.K$, and between $r_b.K$ and $r_{b+1}.K$. Unfortunately, there is as yet no known algebraic function satisfying the additive property for which there is no simple way to derive the inverse function $\mathcal{H}(x)$ for $x \leq 0$. The existence of the inverse function would allow a breached server to return $\mathcal{H}(\alpha - r_{a-1}.K)$ and $\mathcal{H}(r_{b+1}.K - \beta)$ even for $r_{a-1}.K \geq \alpha$ and $r_{b+1}.K \leq \beta$, thus breaking the security of the scheme.

In the absence of a suitable algebraic function, we have to use an iterative hash function instead. Thus, the owner creates the signature for record r_i, $1 \leq i \leq n$, as:

$$sig(r_i) = s(\mathcal{H}(\mathcal{H}^{r_i.K - r_{i-1}.K}(r_{i-1}) \mid \mathcal{H}^{r_{i+1}.K - r_i.K}(r_{i+1}) \mid \mathcal{H}(r_i))), \tag{3.1}$$

where s is a signature function using the owner's private key, $\mathcal{H}^x(r_i)$ applies a collision-resistant hash function $\mathcal{H}$ on (the concatenation of) all the attribute values of record r_i iteratively for x times, and $\mathcal{H}(r_i)$ is the hash digest of the attributes (including K) of r_i.

By using all the record attributes in the input argument for the hash function, a brute-force enumeration of all possible arguments would incur a cost in the order of $2^{|r|}$, where $|r|$ is the record size in bits. At current hardware speed, $|r| = 1024$ bits would be sufficient to render a brute-force attack computationally infeasible. In case the actual attributes total less than 1024 bits, we could simply pad each record with a randomly generated string attribute, at the expense of some storage overhead.

Furthermore, for the boundary records r_0 and r_{n+1}:

$$sig(r_0) = s(\mathcal{H}^{r_1.K-\mathcal{L}}(r_1))$$
$$sig(r_{n+1}) = s(\mathcal{H}^{\mathcal{U}-r_n.K}(r_n)) .$$

2. Query processing

Along with the query answer $\sigma_{K\in[\alpha,\beta]}(\mathbf{R}) = [r_a, .., r_b]$, the server returns the associated record signatures, and intermediate digests $\mathcal{H}^{\alpha-r_{a-1}.K}(r_{a-1})$ and $\mathcal{H}^{r_{b+1}.K-\beta}(r_{b+1})$.

3. Answer verification

Finally, the user checks the signature of each record in $\sigma_{K\in[\alpha,\beta]}(\mathbf{R})$ as follows.

For $sig(r_a)$:

(a) Hash the intermediate digest $\mathcal{H}^{\alpha-r_{a-1}.K}(r_{a-1})$, $(r_a.K - \alpha)$ more times to produce $\mathcal{H}^{r_a.K-r_{a-1}.K}(r_{a-1})$.

(b) Compute $\mathcal{H}^{r_{a+1}.K-r_a.K}(r_{a+1})$ from the value of r_a and r_{a+1} in $\sigma_{K\in[\alpha,\beta]}(\mathbf{R})$.

(c) Compute $\mathcal{H}(r_a)$ from the attribute values of r_a in $\sigma_{K\in[\alpha,\beta]}(\mathbf{R})$.

(d) Check whether:

$$s^{-1}(sig(r_a)) = \mathcal{H}(\mathcal{H}^{r_a.K-r_{a-1}.K}(r_{a-1}) \mid \mathcal{H}^{r_{a+1}.K-r_a.K}(r_{a+1}) \mid \mathcal{H}(r_a)) ,$$

where $s^{-1}(.)$ decrypts its argument with the owner's public key. If so, r_a is indeed the first record that satisfies $\alpha \leq r.K$, and r_a has not been tampered with; otherwise the answer $\sigma_{K\in[\alpha,\beta]}(\mathbf{R})$ is wrong.

For $sig(r_i)$, $a < i < b$:

(a) Compute $\mathcal{H}^{r_i.K-r_{i-1}.K}(r_{i-1})$ from the value of r_{i-1} and r_i in $\sigma_{K\in[\alpha,\beta]}(\mathbf{R})$.

(b) Compute $\mathcal{H}^{r_{i+1}.K-r_i.K}(r_{i+1})$ from the value of r_i and r_{i+1} in $\sigma_{K\in[\alpha,\beta]}(\mathbf{R})$.

(c) Compute $\mathcal{H}(r_i)$ from the attribute values of r_i in $\sigma_{K\in[\alpha,\beta]}(\mathbf{R})$.

(d) Check whether:

$$s^{-1}(sig(r_i)) = \mathcal{H}(\mathcal{H}^{r_i.K-r_{i-1}.K}(r_{i-1}) \mid \mathcal{H}^{r_{i+1}.K-r_i.K}(r_{i+1}) \mid \mathcal{H}(r_i)) .$$

For $sig(r_b)$:

(a) Compute $\mathcal{H}^{r_b.K-r_{b-1}.K}(r_{b-1})$ from the value of r_{b-1} and r_b in $\sigma_{K\in[\alpha,\beta]}(\mathbf{R})$.

(b) Hash the intermediate digest $\mathcal{H}^{r_{b+1}.K-\beta}(r_{b+1})$, $(\beta - r_b.K)$ more times to produce

$\mathcal{H}^{r_{b+1}.K-r_b.K}(r_{b+1})$.

(c) Compute $\mathcal{H}(r_b)$ from the attribute values of r_b in $\sigma_{K\in[\alpha,\beta]}(\mathbf{R})$.

(d) Check whether:

$$s^{-1}(sig(r_b)) = \mathcal{H}(\mathcal{H}^{r_b.K-r_{b-1}.K}(r_{b-1}) \mid \mathcal{H}^{r_{b+1}.K-r_b.K}(r_{b+1}) \mid \mathcal{H}(r_b)).$$

To save on transmission and verification overhead, the signature of all the result tuples may be aggregated into one, and the user may then verify the result tuples together against the aggregate signature, as explained in Section 2.1.

We now explain why the iterative hash functions are applied to r_{i-1} and r_{i+1} in Formula (3.1). If the first iterative hash function there is applied on r_a instead, the server would have to return the intermediate digest $\mathcal{H}^{\alpha-r_{a-1}.K}(r_a)$ to enable the user to check against $sig(r_a)$. As the user knows the value of α, and as r_a is returned to the user as part of the query answer, the user can simply see how many times he has to hash r_a to get a match with the intermediate digest $\mathcal{H}^{\alpha-r_{a-1}.K}(r_a)$, and from there calculate $r_{a-1}.K$. Thus, the key value of r_{a-1} is compromised. Similarly, the key value of r_{b+1} would be compromised if the iterative hash function is applied on r_b rather than r_{b+1} as in Formula (3.1).

In theory, a relation could have several signature chains, one on each sort order of the relation. As the signature chains incur storage and update overheads, they should be applied judiciously, on only the interesting sort orders (as defined by the WHERE clauses in expected queries for which correctness proofs are needed). This is analogous to building indexes only on interesting sort orders, rather than all attribute permutations of a table. At a finer granularity, it is possible to design the server and client software to skip the proof generation and verification protocol for selected queries that do not require proofs, even when an underlying signature chain is available.

Null Query Answer

With the basic signature scheme above, the server cannot drop some valid values or introduce tampered values without being detected by the user. However, extra provisions are still needed for checking null query answers. These provisions necessitate a shadow table for each data table, and should be enabled only if users demand proof for null query answers.

Case 1: $\sigma_{K\in[\alpha,\beta]}(\mathbf{R}) = \emptyset$ because $\beta < r_1.K$.

To prove that $\sigma_{K\in[\alpha,\beta]}(\mathbf{R})$ is correct, the server returns $sig(r_0)$ and the intermediate digest $\mathcal{H}^{r_1.K-\beta}(r_1)$. The user hashes the intermediate digest $(\beta - \mathcal{L})$ more times to produce $\mathcal{H}^{r_1.K-\mathcal{L}}(r_1)$. If and only if it matches $s^{-1}(sig(r_0))$, β is smaller than $r_1.K$ and the null answer is correct.

Case 2: $\sigma_{K\in[\alpha,\beta]}(\mathbf{R}) = \emptyset$ because $r_n.K < \alpha$.

To prove that $\sigma_{K\in[\alpha,\beta]}(\mathbf{R})$ is correct, the server returns $sig(r_{n+1})$ and the intermediate digest $\mathcal{H}^{\alpha-r_n.K}(r_n)$. The user hashes the intermediate digest $(\mathcal{U} - \alpha)$ more times to produce $\mathcal{H}^{\mathcal{U}-r_n.K}(r_n)$. If and only if it matches $s^{-1}(sig(r_{n+1}))$, α is larger than $r_n.K$ and the null answer is correct.

Case 3: $\sigma_{K\in[\alpha,\beta]}(\mathbf{R}) = \emptyset$ because $r_i.K < \alpha \leq \beta < r_{i+1}.K$ for some $1 \leq i < n$.

A straightforward first attempt for proving $\sigma_{K\in[\alpha,\beta]}(\mathbf{R})$ in this case is for the server to return the signature $sig(r_i)$, the digest $\mathcal{H}^{r_i.K-r_{i-1}.K}(r_{i-1})$, the intermediate digest $\mathcal{H}^{r_{i+1}.K-\beta+\alpha-r_i.K}(r_{i+1})$, and the digest $\mathcal{H}(r_i)$. The user will hash the intermediate digest $(\beta - \alpha)$ more times to derive $\mathcal{H}^{r_{i+1}.K-r_i.K}(r_{i+1})$, then check against the signature $sig(r_i)$. Unfortunately, the server could just as well supply the signature and digests for any $1 \leq j < n, i \neq j$, such that $r_{j+1}.K - r_j.K > \beta - \alpha$, and the user verification would still succeed. Thus, the first attempt is not secure.

To handle the present case securely, a shadow table $\mathbf{T} = [t_1, .., t_{n-1}]$ is introduced. Each shadow record $t_i \in \mathbf{T}$ comprises a key K and a signature. $t_i.K$ is set to any value in between those of data records r_i and r_{i+1}, i.e., $r_i.K < t_i.K < r_{i+1}.K$ for $1 \leq i < n$. The signature of t_i is computed as:

$$sig(t_i) = s(\mathcal{H}(\mathcal{H}^{t_i.K-r_i.K}(r_i) \mid \mathcal{H}^{r_{i+1}.K-t_i.K}(r_{i+1}) \mid \mathcal{H}(t_i.K))) . \tag{3.2}$$

For integer domain, we simply leave $sig(t_i)$ undefined whenever $r_i.K = r_{i+1}.K$ or $r_i.K + 1 = r_{i+1}.K$. The reason is that those conditions are incongruent with $r_i.K < \alpha \leq \beta < r_{i+1}.K$.

Along with the query answer, the server returns $t_i.K$, $sig(t_i)$, and the following digests:

> if $(\beta \leq t_i.K)$ then
>> return $\mathcal{H}^{\alpha-r_i.K}(r_i)$, $\mathcal{H}^{\beta-r_i.K}(r_i)$ and $\mathcal{H}^{r_{i+1}.K-t_i.K}(r_{i+1})$;
> else if $(t_i.K \leq \alpha)$ then
>> return $\mathcal{H}^{t_i.K-r_i.K}(r_i)$, $\mathcal{H}^{r_{i+1}.K-\alpha}(r_{i+1})$ and $\mathcal{H}^{r_{i+1}.K-\beta}(r_{i+1})$;
> else // $\alpha < t_i.K < \beta$
>> return $\mathcal{H}^{\alpha-r_i.K}(r_i)$ and $\mathcal{H}^{r_{i+1}.K-\beta}(r_{i+1})$;

Finally, the user combines the digests and checks whether they match the signature:

$$s^{-1}(sig(t_i)) = \mathcal{H}(\mathcal{H}^{t_i.K-r_i.K}(r_i) \mid \mathcal{H}^{r_{i+1}.K-t_i.K}(r_{i+1}) \mid \mathcal{H}(t_i.K)) . \tag{3.3}$$

Specifically, the digests are combined as follows in order to check Equation (3.3):

> if $(\beta \leq t_i.K)$ then
>> hash $\mathcal{H}^{\alpha-r_i.K}(r_i)$ $(t_i.K - \alpha)$ times to get $\mathcal{H}^{t_i.K-r_i.K}(r_i)$;
>> hash $\mathcal{H}^{\beta-r_i.K}(r_i)$ $(t_i.K - \beta)$ times to get $\mathcal{H}^{t_i.K-r_i.K}(r_i)$;
> else if $(t_i.K \leq \alpha)$ then
>> hash $\mathcal{H}^{r_{i+1}.K-\alpha}(r_{i+1})$ $(\alpha - t_i.K)$ times to get $\mathcal{H}^{r_{i+1}.K-t_i.K}(r_{i+1})$;
>> hash $\mathcal{H}^{r_{i+1}.K-\beta}(r_{i+1})$ $(\beta - t_i.K)$ times to get $\mathcal{H}^{r_{i+1}.K-t_i.K}(r_{i+1})$;
> else // $\alpha < t_i.K < \beta$
>> hash $\mathcal{H}^{\alpha-r_i.K}(r_i)$ $(t_i.K - \alpha)$ times to get $\mathcal{H}^{t_i.K-r_i.K}(r_i)$;
>> hash $\mathcal{H}^{r_{i+1}.K-\beta}(r_{i+1})$ $(\beta - t_i.K)$ times to get $\mathcal{H}^{r_{i+1}.K-t_i.K}(r_{i+1})$.

Generalization to Other Attribute Types

Floating Point Attributes

To extend signature chaining beyond the integer domain, a floating point attribute t is represented as a mantissa t_m and an exponent t_e ($t = t_m * 2^{t_e}$) where $0.5 \leq t_m < 1$ or $-1 < t_m \leq -0.5$. The inequality $t \geq c$ for some value $c = c_m * 2^{c_e}$ translates to one of the following conditions:

- $c_m < 0 \leq t_m$;

- $(c_m < 0)$ and $(t_m < 0)$ and $((t_e < c_e)$ or $((t_e = c_e)$ and $(t_m > c_m)))$; or

- $(c_m \geq 0)$ and $(t_m \geq 0)$ and $((t_e > c_e)$ or $((t_e = c_e)$ and $(t_m > c_m)))$.

Floating point attributes can thus be supported with two signature chains, on the integer mantissa and on the integer exponent.

Character String Attributes

Another common attribute type in relational databases is character string. Equality match for character strings, e.g., name = "John Smith", can be supported easily, by hashing the string value to an integer digest before applying the signature chain on the digest. In contrast, ad-hoc prefix matches, e.g., name $\geq$ "John*", entail sorting the table on that string attribute, and building a signature chain on each character position; the attribute in each record can then be compared with the string value given in the query, character-by-character.

3.3   PROJECTION QUERY

Consider a relation **R** with schema $\langle K, A_1, A_2, .., A_m \rangle$ that is sorted on K. The **projection** operation $\pi_{K,A_1,...,A_p}(\mathbf{R}) = \{[r.K, r.A_1, .., r.A_p] \mid r \in \mathbf{R}\}$, for some $1 \leq p \leq m$.

For authentication purposes, the projection operation can filter out any or all of the attributes of **R**, except for the sort key K which the user needs in order to test the query answer for completeness. The server should not return to the user any attribute values in the result tuples that should be filtered out, so as to avoid disclosing sensitive columns and compromising any access control rules. Another reason is that some of the omitted attribute values could be very large, e.g., BLOBs, so sending them to the user would incur unnecessary space and transmission overheads.

Both EMB$^-$ and signature chaining can be extended to support projection easily: In both cases, we only need to redefine the digest of a record r as the root digest of the binary MHT over the attribute values in r; this is denoted as $\mathcal{H}(r) = \mathrm{MHT}(r)$. This way, the server can provide the digest in place of the actual value for those attributes that are projected out, so the user can still compute $\mathrm{MHT}(r)$ without the actual values.

Another issue to consider here is the handling of duplicates in the result $\pi_{K,A_1,...,A_p}(\mathbf{R})$. For some queries, the user may want to retain the duplicates, e.g., for the computation of SUM and AVG. For other queries, the user may wish the server to perform duplicate elimination by specifying the keyword DISTINCT. In the former case, the $\mathrm{MHT}(r)$ component enables the user to uniquely identify each duplicate, so the server cannot omit some duplicates without being detected. In the latter case where duplicates are not needed, the server is still required to present $\mathrm{MHT}(r)$ and the signature $sig(r)$ for each eliminated duplicate r to enable all the signatures for $\pi_{A_1,...,A_p}(\mathbf{R})$ to be checked. Admittedly, this discloses the number of data records underlying each result tuple, which may be undesirable in some situations.

3.4   JOIN QUERY

We now turn our focus to equi-join, the most common class of join queries. Let $\mathbf{R} \bowtie_{R.A=S.B} \mathbf{S}$ denote an equi-join between two relations $\mathbf{R}$ and $\mathbf{S}$ with join condition $\mathbf{R}.A = \mathbf{S}.B$ on their respective attributes A and B. Without loss of generality, we assume that the cardinality of $\mathbf{R}$ is smaller than or equal to that of $\mathbf{S}$, i.e., $|\mathbf{R}| \leq |\mathbf{S}|$.

To prove to the user that the join result is correct, the approach proposed by Pang et al. [2009] is to: (a) apply any selection predicate on $\mathbf{R}$ and project out irrelevant attributes to produce a truncated version $\mathbf{R}'$ with a VO for it; (b) for each record $r \in \mathbf{R}'$ that has matches in $\mathbf{S}$, return r and the matching records in $\mathbf{S}$ along with their correctness proofs; and (c) for each record $r \in \mathbf{R}$ that has no matches in $\mathbf{S}$, return the record identifier rid, A, and a proof that the value of $r.A$ does not exist in $\mathbf{S}.B$. Suppose that a fraction α of the records in $\mathbf{R}$ have matching records in $\mathbf{S}$, whilst the remaining $1 - \alpha$ of them do not. The former class of records is handled like a selection $\sigma_{B=r.A}(\mathbf{S})$. For the latter, we examine two authentication mechanisms. To simplify the presentation below, we assume that $\mathbf{R} = \mathbf{R}'$.

Authenticating with Boundary Values

For each record $r \in \mathbf{R}$ that has no matching $\mathbf{S}$ record, the method by Narasimha and Tsudik [2006] returns the boundary $\mathbf{S}.B$ values before and after $r.A$. We denote this method as BV. In the worst case, BV requires two boundary values per r. Where the records in $\mathbf{R}$ share the same boundaries, the duplicated $\mathbf{S}.B$ values can be eliminated to reduce transmission overhead. For example, for two consecutive records $r_1, r_2 \in \mathbf{R}$, $r_1.A$'s upper boundary in $\mathbf{S}$ may be $r_2.A$'s lower boundary. After duplicate elimination, the expected size of all the boundary values from $\mathbf{S}$ that are needed for the proof is

$$|VO|_{BV} = (1 - \alpha)I_A \cdot \min(2, \frac{I_B}{I_A}) \cdot |\mathbf{S}.B| , \qquad (3.4)$$

where I_A and I_B are the number of distinct values in $\mathbf{R}.A$ and $\mathbf{S}.B$ respectively, and $|\mathbf{S}.B|$ is the size (in bytes) of the $\mathbf{S}.B$ attribute. Note that this formula refers only to the part of the proof for records in $\mathbf{R}$ which have no matching counterparts in $\mathbf{S}$. Due to these records, the VO size is expected to be huge.

Authenticating with Bloom Filters

The second authentication mechanism is developed by Pang et al. [2009]. Denoted as BF, it returns a certified Bloom filter [Bloom, 1970] on $\mathbf{S}.B$, for the user to test those unmatched $\mathbf{R}$ records in the query answer.

Suppose that an m-bit Bloom filter is constructed for the I_B distinct values in $\mathbf{S}.B$. The expected false positive rate is $FP = 0.6185^{m/I_B}$ (according to Formula (2.1)). Where the Bloom filter gives a negative, the corresponding $\mathbf{R}$ record is certain not to have a match in $\mathbf{S}$, and no additional proof is needed. Where a false positive occurs for some $r.A$, the server needs to return the two corresponding boundary values from $\mathbf{S}.B$. Since the Bloom filter is unlikely to produce false positives for consecutive $\mathbf{R}$ records, there can be no significant improvement from duplicate elimination. Hence, the expected size of the proof for the $(1 - \alpha)$ unmatched fraction of $\mathbf{R}$ is

$\frac{m}{8} + (1 - \alpha)I_A \cdot FP \cdot 2|S.B|$ bytes – the first term is the Bloom filter size, while the second term accounts for the boundary values for proving the unmatched **R** records that get a false positive on the filter.

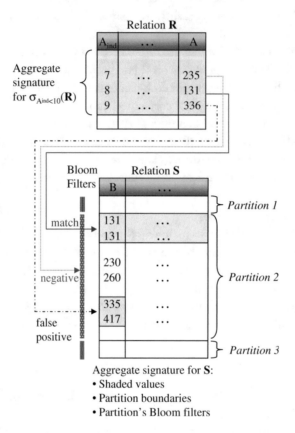

Figure 3.5: Authenticated equi-join with Bloom filters.

Figure 3.5 illustrates how an equi-join $\sigma_{A_{ind}<10}(\mathbf{R}) \bowtie_{A=B} \mathbf{S}$ is authenticated with a Bloom filter. First, the range of **R** records that satisfy $\mathbf{R}.A_{ind} < 10$ are gathered as part of the query answer. To allow the user to verify this part of the answer, those **R** records' signatures are combined into an aggregate signature $ASign_R$. Some of those **R** records, e.g., $\langle 8, \ldots, 131 \rangle$, have matching records in **S**; the matching **S** records are added to the query answer. To prove that the rest of the **R** records do not have matching **S** records, the certified Bloom filter (constructed by the owner beforehand) is supplied to the user. **R** records like $\langle 7, \ldots, 235 \rangle$ test negative on the Bloom filter, which suffices to convince the user that there is no **S** record with $S.B = 235$. The remaining **R** records (such as $\langle 9, \ldots, 336 \rangle$) give a false positive on the Bloom filter, and need to be proven by inspecting the adjoining boundary **S** records (with $S.B = 335$ and $S.B = 417$). The signatures for the matching

S records, the boundary **S** records, and the Bloom filter are combined into an aggregate signature $ASign_S$. Finally, $ASign_R$ and $ASign_S$ are aggregated to produce the signature for the query answer.

Although the above mechanism is adequate for proving unmatched **R** records, there is a shortcoming. This is because new data can be added easily to a Bloom filter, but it is not possible to remove the effect of a record from the filter. Consequently, following every record deletion, the Bloom filter has to be reconstructed from the remaining records, which is very expensive for large datasets.

To limit the update overhead, **S** is split so that a Bloom filter can be created per partition, rather than just a single filter for the entire **S**. Continuing the illustration in Figure 3.5, **S** is sorted on **S**.B, and partitioned horizontally into the ranges $[0, 120)$, $[120, 420)$ and $[420, 1000)$. The finer the partitions, the lower the update cost. However, there is an upper bound to the number of partitions beyond which the Bloom filter mechanism becomes more expensive than simply returning all the boundary values in **S**.B.

Suppose that **S**.B is divided into p partitions. For a given query, those partition filters that are probed by unmatched **R** records are returned, along with the corresponding partition boundaries. Where adjoining partitions are returned, we can again avoid duplicating their common boundaries in the VO. This brings the proof size to

$$|VO|_{BF} = (1-\alpha)\frac{m}{8} + min(1, 2(1-\alpha)) \cdot p\,|\mathbf{S}.B| \qquad (3.5)$$
$$+ (1-\alpha)I_A \cdot FP \cdot 2\,|\mathbf{S}.B|,$$

where m is the total size (in bits) of the partition filters. The first term above corresponds to the total size of the partition filters that are probed by unmatched **R** records. The second term accounts for the partition boundaries. If only a few partitions are probed, the server sends their lower and upper boundaries (thus, $2(1-\alpha) \cdot p\,|\mathbf{S}.B|$); whereas if most of them are probed, it is cheaper to return all the boundaries (thus, $p\,|\mathbf{S}.B|$). The third term is due to those unmatched **R** records that get a false positive, and hence need to be authenticated via boundary **S** records. We want $|VO|_{BF}$ to be lower than $|VO|_{BV}$, thus:

$$\frac{m}{8|\mathbf{S}.B|} < I_A\left[min(2, \frac{I_B}{I_A}) - 2\,FP\right] - \frac{min(1, 2(1-\alpha))\,p}{1-\alpha}. \qquad (3.6)$$

To analyze the implications of the above condition, we first consider the case of a primary key **R**.A to foreign key **S**.B join between **R** and **S**. The primary key-foreign key relationship requires every **S**.B value to exist in **R**.A, so $I_A \geq I_B$. Assuming that $|\mathbf{S}.B|$ occupies 4 bytes, and setting $m = 8I_B$ (meaning the partition filters are configured with 8 bits per distinct **S**.B value) so that $FP = 0.0216$, Formula 3.6 becomes:

$$0.75\,I_B - 0.0432\,I_A - \frac{min(1, 2(1-\alpha)) \cdot p}{1-\alpha} > 0. \qquad (3.7)$$

A sufficient condition that satisfies the above inequality is $0.75\,I_B > 0.0432\,I_A + 2p$, or equivalently $z = 0.0432\frac{I_A}{I_B} + 2\frac{p}{I_B} < 0.75$. Figure 3.6 depicts the condition, with the blue surface

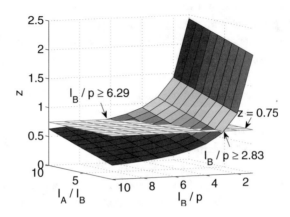

Figure 3.6: Configuration for join processing with Bloom filters.

under the white plane at $z = 0.75$ demarcating the viable $\frac{I_A}{I_B}$ and $\frac{I_B}{p}$ settings. According to the figure, we need $\frac{I_B}{p} \geq 2.83$ if $\frac{I_A}{I_B} = 1$, and $\frac{I_B}{p} \geq 6.29$ at $\frac{I_A}{I_B} = 10$. This means that a higher $\frac{I_A}{I_B}$ ratio requires each partition to contain proportionally more distinct $\mathbf{S}.B$ values. This requirement should not pose a difficulty in practice. Suppose that $\mathbf{S}$ is indexed with a B^+-tree. Given that a B^+-tree typically has a fan-out of a few hundred, each leaf node can be a partition with its own Bloom filter, and the inequality in Formula 3.7 will still be satisfied for a wide spectrum of join queries. Such a granularity is also I/O-efficient, because the Bloom filter for an updated leaf node is written back to disk along with the leaf node in a single I/O operation. For memory-resident indexes that typically have small fan-out factors, a partition may span multiple leaf nodes in order to satisfy the constraint on p.

Now consider the case where $\mathbf{R}.A$ and $\mathbf{S}.B$ are not a primary key-foreign key pair; instead, $\mathbf{R} \bowtie_{\mathbf{R}.A=\mathbf{S}.B} \mathbf{S}$ is merely an arbitrary equi-join operation. If $I_A \geq I_B$, the earlier analysis is still applicable, so we shall focus on the situation where $I_A < I_B$. If $\frac{I_B}{I_A} > 2$, Formula (3.6) becomes $1.9568\frac{I_A}{I_B} - \frac{min(1,2(1-\alpha))}{1-\alpha} \cdot \frac{p}{I_B} > 0.25$, again assuming that $|\mathbf{S}.B| = 4, m = 8I_B$ and $FP = 0.0216$. A sufficient condition for the inequality to hold is $0.9784\frac{I_A}{I_B} - \frac{p}{I_B} > 0.125$. Since $\frac{p}{I_B} > 0$, the constraint indicates that the BF method is not beneficial to any equi-join where $I_B \geq 7.8272\,I_A$. This is intuitive since the Bloom filters must then be configured with a large m in order to achieve the desired $\frac{m}{I_B}$ ratio and hence false positive rate, making the filters overly bulky and costly to transmit to the user.

3.5   AGGREGATION QUERY

The signature chaining technique that we introduced in Section 3.2.3 can be applied for authenticating single-attribute range aggregate queries of the form SELECT SUM(S) FROM $\mathbf{R}$ WHERE $\alpha \leq K \leq \beta$ for attributes S and K in $\mathbf{R}$. We first present the solution by Pang and Tan [2008] for the range sum query, and discuss extension to other aggregation functions at the end of the section. Support for GROUP BY is discussed in Section 3.5.3.

We assume that a user who has access right to pose an aggregate query over a given range of records, $\alpha \leq K \leq \beta$, is also allowed to aggregate over any sub-interval within $[\alpha, \beta]$. By extension, the user can access the underlying record values that contribute to the aggregate. However, the user chooses not to retrieve the underlying data directly due to resource considerations, for instance because the user device is resource-constrained, or to minimize network traffic. Instead, the user relies on the server to compute the aggregate. Obviously, this approach makes sense only if the cost of verifying the aggregate answer is much lower than the cost of retrieving the underlying data directly for user inspection. In the case where the user is not authorized to inspect the underlying data, a trusted intermediary has to be enlisted to produce the correct aggregate result, or to verify the correctness of the answer produced by the server.

3.5.1   PARTIAL SUM HIERARCHY

At one extreme, a range aggregate query could be satisfied by returning all the underlying record values. After verifying that the returned values are authentic and complete, using any of the range selection authentication mechanisms in Section 3.2, the user then computes the aggregate herself. With this approach, the network transmission and client computation are proportional to the number of records in the query range. These overheads are very high, considering that the user desires just a single aggregate value.

From the user's perspective, ideally the server should return a single certified value for the aggregate query. This is possible if the owner pre-computes and signs every range aggregate. Without prior knowledge of the query range, the owner has to materialize all $n!$ possible range aggregates for a table of n records. Clearly, the computation and storage overheads are prohibitive. As a compromise, the server can return a list of certified partial sums corresponding to partitions of the query range.

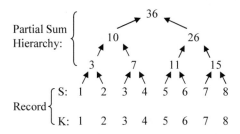

Figure 3.7: Partial sum hierarchy with fan-out $f = 2$.

The solution by Pang and Tan [2008] requires the owner to materialize a hierarchy of partial sums over the records, as Figure 3.7 demonstrates. The size of the query answer can be reduced by returning partial sums corresponding to the largest partitions that together cover the query range.

The partial sum hierarchy that has to be maintained by the owner and the server has approximately $2n - 1$ nodes.

Let us now consider the number of values that are returned to the user. We shall call the smallest subtree in the partial sum hierarchy that encompasses the query range the *covering subtree*. We first consider the case where the left boundary of the query range is aligned with the leftmost record of the covering subtree, e.g., the range selection $1 \leq K \leq 6$ on the data set in Figure 3.7. Here, the first 2^2 records are aggregated into a partial sum 10, and the next 2^1 records are aggregated into another partial sum 11. Denote the binary representation of the query answer size (i.e., number of records in the query range) q as $q = \sum_{i=0}^{\lfloor log_2 q \rfloor} b_i \cdot 2^i$, $b_i = 0$ or 1. Starting from $i = \lfloor log_2 q \rfloor$ down to 0, from the left boundary of the query range towards the right, 2^i records in the query range are aggregated into a partial sum if $b_i = 1$. Thus, the number of returned partial sums is $\sum_{i=0}^{\lfloor log_2 q \rfloor} b_i$, and is at most $\lfloor log_2 q \rfloor + 1$. The case where the right boundary of the query range is aligned with the rightmost record of the covering subtree, e.g., the range selection $3 \leq K \leq 8$ on the data set, is similar to the first case. If both the left and right boundaries of the query range are not aligned with the edges of the covering subtree, the query range is decomposed into up to $2(\lfloor log_2 \frac{q}{2} \rfloor + 1)$ partitions and hence partial sums. For example, for the range selection $2 \leq K \leq 7$, the query answer comprises the datum 2, the partial sums 7 and 11, followed by the datum 7.

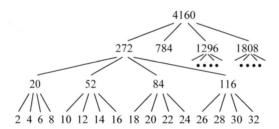

Figure 3.8: Partial sum hierarchy with $f = 4$.

The partial sum hierarchy can be generalized to have a fan-out of $f > 1$, i.e., each node in the hierarchy aggregates f child nodes. With this general scheme, the partial sum hierarchy contains approximately $\frac{fn-1}{f-1}$ nodes. Figure 3.8 illustrates a partial sum hierarchy with $n=16$ and $f=4$. Consider again the case where the left boundary of the query range is aligned with the leftmost record of the covering subtree, e.g., the range selection $2 \leq K \leq 13$ on the data set in Figure 3.8. Denote the query answer size q with the polynomial $q = \sum_{i=0}^{\lfloor log_f q \rfloor} b_i \cdot f^i$, $0 \leq b_i < f$. Starting from $i = \lfloor log_f q \rfloor$ down to 0, from the left boundary of the query range towards the right, $b_i \cdot f^i$ records in the query range are aggregated into b_i partial sums. Hence, the number of partial sums returned is

$$\text{\# partial sums} = \sum_{i=0}^{\lfloor log_f q \rfloor} b_i \qquad (3.8)$$

and at the most there are

$$\text{max \# partial sums} = (f - 1) \cdot (\lfloor log_f q \rfloor + 1) \tag{3.9}$$

partial sums in the query answer. If both the left and right boundaries of the query range are not aligned with the edges of the covering subtree, the query range is decomposed into up to $2(f - 1)(\lfloor log_f \frac{q}{2} \rfloor + 1)$ partial sums. For example, for the range selection $8 \leq K \leq 29$, the query answer size comprises the record value 8, the partial sums 52 and 84, followed by the record values 26 and 28.

Formula (3.9) confirms that the approach of producing partial sums scales better than returning the underlying record values to the user directly, which would have generated query answer sizes that are proportional to q.

3.5.2 CERTIFIED PARTIAL SUM HIERARCHY

Having introduced the partial sum hierarchy for computing range aggregates, we now explain how Pang and Tan [2008] built authentication information into the scheme. There are two primary considerations for proving the correctness of a range aggregate result: each returned partial sum is an accurate aggregation of the records in its scope, and together the returned partial sums cover all the records in the query range.

Since the owner is secure in our system model, the owner can generate a signature for each partial sum based on its value. Whenever a partial sum is returned to the user, the server produces the associated signature to prove that it has not been tampered with. Besides the value of the partial sum, the signature construction also includes the record immediately below and the record immediately above the scope of the partial sum (i.e., using the signature chaining technique introduced in Section 3.2.3). This enables the user to confirm that the partial sums in a query answer provide continuous coverage of the query range, by simply checking that the record just above the scope of one partial sum is indeed the first record in the next partial sum. The detailed formulation is as follows.

Given a set of records, each having the attributes $\langle K, S, A \rangle$ where K is the key attribute for the range selection, S is the attribute to be aggregated, and A denotes the remaining record values, sort the records on K, then construct a partial sum hierarchy over the records. (The construction algorithm will be given shortly.) Every partition in the hierarchy has up to f child pointers p_i, each with the attributes listed in Table 3.1.

The signature for each partition, $p_i.\text{sign}$, is pre-computed by the owner for distribution to the server along with the data, using the formula:

$$p_i.\text{sign} = s(\mathcal{H}(\mathcal{H}^{p_i.K_l - p_i.r_l.K}(\mathcal{H}(p_i.r_l)) \mid p_i.K_l \mid p_i.K_h \mid p_i.\text{psum} \mid \tag{3.10}$$
$$\mathcal{H}^{p_i.r_h.K - p_i.K_h}(\mathcal{H}(p_i.r_h)))),$$

where s signs its argument with the owner's private key, and $\mathcal{H}^x(y)$ hashes y iteratively for x times. Furthermore, $p_i.r_l$ and $p_i.r_h$ are the records immediately below and above the coverage of p_i, respectively. For example, for the partition anchored at node 52 in Figure 3.8, the

Table 3.1: Attributes of child pointer p_i in the partial sum hierarchy.

Parameter	Description	Size
ptr	Points to a sub-partition within p_i (bytes)	4
K_l	Key value of the leftmost record covered by p_i (bytes)	4
K_h	Key value of the rightmost record covered by p_i (bytes)	4
D_l	Digest from applying a one-way hash function $\mathcal{H}$ on the first record in partition p_i (bytes)	16
D_h	Digest from applying $\mathcal{H}$ on the last record in p_i (bytes)	16
psum	Partial sum of the records covered by p_i (bytes)	8
sign	Signature for p_i (bytes)	128
	Total pointer size (bytes)	180

records below and above its coverage are 8 and 18 respectively, so its signature is derived as $s(\mathcal{H}(\mathcal{H}^{10-8}(\mathcal{H}(8)) \mid 10 \mid 16 \mid 52 \mid \mathcal{H}^{18-16}(\mathcal{H}(18))))$ (assuming for simplicity that each record contains only its key value, i.e., $r_i = r_i.K$).

For a range aggregate query, the returned answer contains a list of partitions $\{p_a, p_{a+1}, .., p_b\}$, each having the format $\langle K_l, K_h, D_l, D_h, \text{psum}, \text{sign} \rangle$. To minimize transmission and storage overheads, D_l and D_h are returned in place of the actual records.

In verifying each partition p_i in the query answer, the user checks whether:

$$s^{-1}(p_i.\text{sign}) = \mathcal{H}(\mathcal{H}^{p_i.K_l - p_{i-1}.K_h}(p_{i-1}.D_h) \mid p_i.K_l \mid p_i.K_h \mid p_i.\text{psum} \mid \tag{3.11}$$
$$\mathcal{H}^{p_{i+1}.K_l - p_i.K_h}(p_{i+1}.D_l)) ,$$

where s^{-1} decrypts the given signature with the owner's public key.

The first term in Formula (3.10), $\mathcal{H}^{p_i.K_l - p_i.r_l.K}(\mathcal{H}(p_i.r_l))$, matches the first term in Formula (3.11), $\mathcal{H}^{p_i.K_l - p_{i-1}.K_h}(p_{i-1}.D_h)$, only if the record just below p_i's coverage ($p_i.r_l$) is the same record that hashes to $p_{i-1}.D_h$, otherwise there is a collision in the collision-resistant hash function $\mathcal{H}$. This proves that partition p_i's coverage begins right after the preceding partition p_{i-1} in the query answer. Likewise, the last term $\mathcal{H}^{p_{i+1}.K_l - p_i.K_h}(p_{i+1}.D_l)$ in Formula (3.11) is for verifying that p_i's coverage ends just before the subsequent partition p_{i+1} in the query answer.

Besides ensuring contiguous coverage of the query range by the partitions in the answer, the user will also want to ascertain that the first partition p_a in the answer starts from the first qualifying record. Equivalently, the record immediately below p_a should have a smaller key value than the query range, i.e., $p_a.r_l.K < \alpha$. This is achieved by having the server return an intermediate digest $\mathcal{H}^{\alpha - p_a.r_l.K}(\mathcal{H}(p_a.r_l))$, which the user then hashes $p_a.K_l - \alpha$ more times to produce the first term in Formula (3.11). Since the intermediate digest is defined only for positive number of iterations of $\mathcal{H}$, p_a's signature can be matched only if indeed $p_a.r_l.K < \alpha$. Similarly, the server can prove that the record immediately after the last partition p_b satisfies $p_b.r_h.K > \beta$.

In proving that the query answer covers the query range completely, we have to be careful that the proof does not leak information about records beyond the query range. In particular, the intermediate digest $\mathcal{H}^{\alpha - p_a.r_l.K}(\mathcal{H}(p_a.r_l))$ should not compromise $p_a.r_l$. Since α originated from the user, $\mathcal{H}(p_a.r_l)$ should not be released also to the user, otherwise the user can deduce $p_a.r_l.K$ by counting the number of times that $\mathcal{H}(p_a.r_l)$ needs to be hashed in order to match the intermediate digest.

3.5.3   QUERY PROCESSING USING THE PARTIAL SUM HIERARCHY

Aggregate with range predicate

A single-attribute range sum has the form SELECT SUM(S) FROM **R** WHERE $\alpha \leq K \leq \beta$. This query is processed by traversing down the root of the partial sum hierarchy, along progressively finer partitions that contain the query range, till we reach the covering subtree. Recall that the covering subtree is the smallest subtree in the partial sum hierarchy that encompasses the query range $K \in [\alpha, \beta]$. For example, for the range selection $8 \leq K \leq 29$ on the data set in Figure 3.8, the server traverses from the root (4160) to reach the partial sum (272) that anchors the covering subtree. The partial sums (52 and 84) within the covering subtree aggregate the records in the middle of the query range. To complete the query answer, the server iteratively retrieves record values or partial sums, on the next level down the hierarchy, that aggregate the records toward the left and right boundaries of the query range. In our current example, this step elicits the record values 8 on the left, and 26 and 28 on the right. Together, the retrieved records values and partial sums effectively form a "canopy" over the query range.

Aggregate with GROUP BY

This query has the form SELECT SUM(S) FROM **R** GROUP BY K. The result comprises a list of sums, one for each $k_i \in K$. Each sum, in turn, is made up of a list of record values and partial sums, as with a range sum query over $[k_i, k_i]$. The user needs to verify that the last record in the scope of a sum is the immediate neighbor of the first record in the scope of the following sum, using Formula (3.11).

Signature Aggregation

The overheads of transmitting and verifying a signature for every partial sum in the answer for a range aggregation can be very large. Instead, the server can combine the signatures for the individual partial sums into one aggregated signature, using techniques in Section 2.1, so that there is only one signature verification per query answer.

3.5.4   DATA ORGANIZATION

As shown in Table 3.1, each child pointer in the partial sum hierarchy has the attributes $\langle$ptr, K_l, K_h, D_l, D_h, psum, sign$\rangle$, with a total length of 180 bytes. If these attributes are stored within the partial sum hierarchy, each node can only hold at most 22 child pointers, assuming a typical block size of 4 Kbytes. A table containing just 10 million records would thus generate a partial sum hierarchy with a height of 6.

An alternate data organization is to store all the pointer attributes outside of the partial sum hierarchy, in a separate *PtrAttr* file. With this organization, the partial sum hierarchy can be simplified to a conventional B$^+$-tree, in which each node is augmented with an offset into the *PtrAttr* file where the attribute values of the node's child pointers are located. Assuming 4 bytes each for the file offset, child pointers and key values in a tree node, a 4-Kbyte block allows a fan-out f of around 510. Thus, a table with 10 million records requires only a B$^+$-tree height of 3, half of the height for the previous organization where the attribute values are stored within the hierarchy. In actual deployment, the realizable I/O savings could be even higher, as the top 2 layers of the tree/hierarchy are usually buffered. In addition, the following observations can be exploited to optimize the structure of the *PtrAttr* file, with the aim of reducing the number of random I/Os in favor of sequential I/Os.

(a) If the partial sum for a subtree in the hierarchy is utilized, no descendant partial sums/record values within that subtree will be retrieved by the same query. The converse is also true. For example, in the answer $\{8, 52, 84, 26, 28\}$ for the range aggregate over $8 \leq K \leq 29$ in Figure 3.8, there is no ancestor-descendant relationship between the result entries. It is therefore not beneficial to cluster together attribute values belonging to ancestor and descendant nodes.

(b) Within any node along the canopy over the query range, several of the partial sums are likely to be required for the query answer. For example, $\{52, 84\}$ and $\{26, 28\}$. For this reason, the attribute values of child pointers within the same node should be stored contiguously so that they can be retrieved through sequential I/Os, and the *PtrAttr* file can be structured as a series of buckets that are $176f$ bytes each. (Excluding the child ptr which remains in the partial sum hierarchy, the remaining attributes in Table 3.1 have a combined size of 176 bytes.) With this layout, insertions and deletions to a node propagate only to the corresponding bucket in the *PtrAttr* file; there is no need for sophisticated file management like compaction and shifting of file content. There is also the additional advantage that only one file offset is allocated for each tree node, so the concomitant reduction in fan-out f is negligible.

(c) The canopy over a query range contains nodes along the boundaries of adjacent subtrees. For example, $\{\ldots 32, 784 \ldots\}$, $\{\ldots 116, 784 \ldots\}$ and $\{\ldots 272, 784 \ldots\}$ are all possible canopies in Figure 3.8. It may therefore be tempting to try to store adjacent nodes consecutively. However, without prior knowledge of the workload, there is no objective basis to choose between alternative pairings, e.g., whether 32, 116 or 272 should be selected to precede 784.

Figure 3.9 shows an order-2 B$^+$-tree and the associated *PtrAttr* file for the example in Figure 3.8.

3.5.5   EXTENSION TO OTHER AGGREGATION FUNCTIONS

The partial sum hierarchy has application beyond the SUM function. Gray et al. [1997] defined three classes of aggregation functions: Distributive aggregates can be computed by aggregating the partial aggregates on partitions of the dataset, and include COUNT, SUM, MIN and MAX. Algebraic aggregates are derived from a scalar function of distributive aggregates. For example, AVG can be expressed as SUM / COUNT. In contrast, holistic aggregates like MEDIAN cannot be computed through a divide-and-conquer strategy on the underlying dataset.

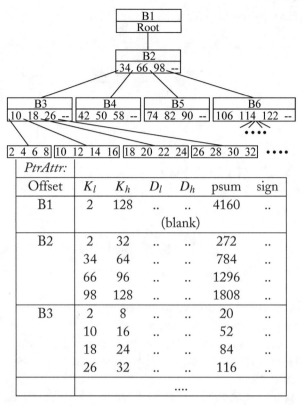

Figure 3.9: Data organization.

The authenticated partial sum hierarchy applies to distributive aggregates and algebraic aggregates in general, by simply substituting the SUM function with the desired aggregation function. However, the solution does not extend to holistic aggregates.

3.5.6   OTHER TECHNIQUES RELATED TO AGGREGATION QUERY

There have been several studies on efficiently evaluating range aggregate queries, particularly in the context of OLAP systems. However, they are not directly applicable to the system model for data publication, as they either leak extra information or they do not support authentication of query answers.

The classic HAMS scheme [Ho et al., 1997] for OLAP range sum works as follows. Consider a data cube with d dimensions, and n_j elements along dimension j. $S[i_1, i_2, ..., i_d]$ denotes the value in cell $[i_1, i_2, ..., i_d]$, and Region$(l_1 : h_1, l_2 : h_2, ..., l_d : h_d)$ denotes the d-dimensional space bounded by $l_j \leq i_j \leq h_j$ along every dimension j. HAMS uses a d-dimensional array P of size

$n_1 \times n_2 \times ... \times n_d$ to store pre-computed prefix sums:

$$P[x_1, x_2, ..., x_d] = \text{SUM}(0 : x_1, 0 : x_2, ..., 0 : x_d)$$
$$= \sum_{i_1=0}^{x_1} \sum_{i_2=0}^{x_2} ... \sum_{i_d=0}^{x_d} S[i_1, i_2, ..., i_d] .$$

At runtime, any range sum can be computed from P as:

$$\text{SUM}(l_1 : h_1, l_2 : h_2, ..., l_d : h_d) =$$
$$\sum_{\forall x_j \in \{l_j-1, h_j\}} \left\{ \left(\prod_{i=1}^{d} s(i) \right) \times P[x_1, x_2, ..., x_d] \right\}, \forall j \in \{1, 2, ..., d\} ,$$

where

$$s(j) = \begin{cases} 1 & \text{if } x_j = h_j \\ -1 & \text{if } x_j = l_j - 1 \end{cases} .$$

For example, when $d = 2$, the range sum is obtained as: $P[h_1, h_2] - P[h_1, l_2 - 1] - P[l_1 - 1, h_2] + P[l_1 - 1, l_2 - 1]$.

The HAMS scheme produces overheads and query answer size that are proportional to 2^d. Moreover, $2^d - 1$ of the prefix sums in the answer relate to records that are outside of the query scope, which violates our minimality requirement. Subsequent extensions to the prefix sum approach, e.g., [Chun et al., 2001] and [Geffner et al., 2000], have focused on reducing update overheads but not authentication considerations.

Przydatek et al. [2003] described an authentication scheme for sensor networks in which aggregators are entrusted with summarizing sensor data for a home server. In the specific case of an "average" operation, the aggregator A commits to the sensor data collection, then reports its average $\bar{x}$ to the home server H. In addition, A sorts the sensor data and commits to the sorted list as well. H then tests whether the two lists contain the same elements through sampling. If the test succeeds, A sends to H the frequency count of each sensor value (or each range of values). Finally, H computes the average directly from the frequency counts, and compares it with $\bar{x}$. This solution does not address our problem of aggregate authentication: (a) Our system model includes a trusted owner that can certify the dataset. There is no necessity, nor is it practical to maintain two lists of the dataset for counterchecking. (b) The frequency counts constitute a histogram of the data distribution. For a large dataset, the histogram has to be pre-generated, and that allows a breached query server to determine the maximum error it can introduce while eluding detection. (c) A large dataset is likely to reside on disk, in a series of physical blocks. Spot checks against the sorted list generate random I/Os and are expensive.

3.6   SUMMARY

In this chapter, we introduced methods for authenticating the answers of several relational operations, including range selection, projection, equi-join, and range aggregation. The methods build upon, and derive their security properties from, standard cryptographic protocols, especially Merkle Hash Tree and signature aggregation.

While existing methods are effective for range selection and projection, the same cannot be said for equi-join and aggregation. In the case of equi-join, the mechanism presented in Section 3.4 is liable to producing a large verification object for a join. In the case of aggregation, the partial sum hierarchy in Section 3.5 entails significant update overheads. Hence, there is scope for further research on these two operations. Finally, the existing authentication mechanisms work only for individual operations; significant challenges remain to be overcome before we have an authentication framework for general SQL queries.

CHAPTER 4

Spatial Queries

There are many applications that manipulate spatial data. For example, Geographic Information Systems (GIS) represent locations as points, rivers and highways as lines and lakes and cities as regions. As another example, in image databases (e.g., satellite images, MRI images, fingerprints), images are typically mapped into feature vectors (which are essentially multi-dimensional points) to facilitate similarity search. More recently, location-based services acquire and manage locations of large quantity of moving objects. In fact, we can also view a traditional relation with k attributes as a collection of k-dimensional points.

Spatial databases are outsourced for various reasons [Yang et al., 2009]. First, this may be the only option to utilize the data. For example, the owner of the data (the organizations that collect the data) may not have the capability to support spatial query services which are typically more challenging than traditional business like services. Second, even if the owner has the ability to manipulate spatial data, it may still be cheaper to outsource to a third party. Finally, many applications (and hence end-users) may benefit from the outsourced data. For example, location data can be combined with online maps to provide directions to guide drivers. This effectively increases the value of the data.

In this chapter, we shall look at mechanisms to authenticate a variety of spatial queries when a spatial database is outsourced including window, range, k-nearest-neighbor (kNN) and reverse NN queries. These methods build authentication information into a spatial data structure such as the R-tree [Guttman, 1984], KD-tree [Bentley, 1975] and iDistance [Yu et al., 2001], from which verification objects can be constructed during query processing for users to verify the query answers.

4.1   BACKGROUND

The general setting of our spatial query authentication problem is as follows. A data owner of a multi-dimensional dataset $\mathcal{DB}$ outsources the management of $\mathcal{DB}$ to a third-party publisher. Besides $\mathcal{DB}$, (s)he also creates one or several associated signatures of $\mathcal{DB}$ that are outsourced together with it. Users are also made aware of certain meta-data, as well as the public key of the owner. During query processing, the publisher returns the answers and the associated *verification objects* (VOs) for the users to verify the correctness of the answers. In particular, the users would like to have the following guarantees in their answers.

- Completeness: The user can verify that all the data points that satisfy a query are included in the answer.

- Authenticity: The user can check that all the values in a query answer originated from the data owner. They have not been tampered with, nor have spurious data points been introduced.

- Minimality: Proving the correctness of a query answer entails minimal disclosure of data points that are beyond the query answers. Ideally, only query answers are returned, and the users cannot derive any non-answer points from the meta-data or verification objects. This property is highly desirable as it facilitates confidentiality without violating access control.

We assume a d-dimensional data space. Let $L = (L_1, L_2, \ldots, L_d)$ and $U = (U_1, U_2, \ldots, U_d)$ be two points that bound the entire d-dimensional data space, where $L_r \leq U_r$ for all r. L and U are known to all users. Suppose the space contains N data points given by $\mathcal{DB} = \{p_1, p_2, \ldots, p_N\}$. We also denote $p_i = (x_{i1}, x_{i2}, \ldots, x_{id})$. We consider the following spatial query types.

- **Window query.** Let $p_l = (x_{l1}, x_{l2}, \ldots, x_{ld})$ and $p_u = (x_{u1}, x_{u2}, \ldots, x_{ud})$ be two points in the data space. A window query, $Q_w = [q_l, q_u]$, returns all points within the hyper-rectangle determined by the two bounding points in Q_W In other words, a point $p_i = (x_{i1}, x_{i2}, \ldots, x_{id})$ is in the answer if $x_{lj} \leq x_{ij} \leq x_{uj}$ for $1 \leq j \leq d$.

- **Range query.** Let $p_c = (x_{c1}, x_{c2}, \ldots, x_{cd})$. A range query $Q_r = [p_c, r]$ returns all points bounded by the hyper-sphere centered at p_c with radius r. In other words, a point $p_i = (x_{i1}, x_{i2}, \ldots, x_{id})$ is in the answer if $dist(p_c, p_i) \leq r$, where $dist(x, y)$ is a function that computes the Euclidean distance between two points x and y.

- **kNN query.** Let $p_c = (x_{c1}, x_{c2}, \ldots, x_{cd})$. A kNN query $Q_k = [p_c, k]$ returns k points $\mathcal{A} = \{q_1, q_2, \ldots, q_k\}$ such that[1]

$$\forall q_i \in \mathcal{A}, \forall p_j \in \mathcal{DB} - \mathcal{A}, dist(p_c, q_i) < dist(p_c, p_j).$$

- **RNN query.** Let $p_c = (x_{c1}, x_{c2}, \ldots, x_{cd})$. An RNN query RNN($p_c$) returns all points that have p_c as their nearest neighbor, i.e.,

$$RNN(p_c) = \{p \in \mathcal{DB} | \forall p_j \in \mathcal{DB} - \{p\}, dist(p, p_c) < dist(p, p_j)\}.$$

As an example, consider a dataset containing 20 data points, r_1 to r_{20}, in a 2-dimensional space as shown in Figure 4.1. The figure shows a window query Q_w for which $\{r_{13}, r_{14}\}$ is the correct result. A rogue publisher may return a wrong result $\{r_{13}, r_{14}, r_{100}\}$, which includes a spurious point r_{100}, or $\{r_{13^*}, r_{14}\}$ in which some attribute values of r_{13} have been tampered with. To detect such incorrect values, the user should be able to verify the *authenticity* of the query result. A different threat is that the publisher may omit some result points, for example by returning only $\{r13\}$ for query Q_w. This threat relates to the *completeness* of query result. Now, the publisher may also return

---

[1]In the case that the kth point and the $(k + 1)$th point are equi-distant from the query point, then both points will be returned.

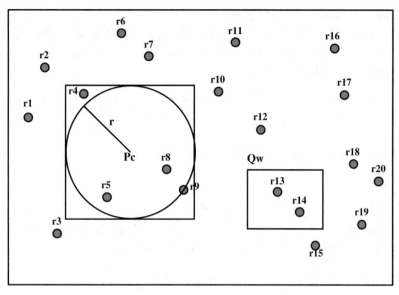

Figure 4.1: Sample queries on a 2-dimensional dataset (a running example).

$\{r_{13}, r_{14}, r_{15}\}$. While the user can verify that r_{15} is a non-answer point that has not been tampered with, revealing r_{15} potentially compromises access control. Instead, it would be ideal to simply return $\{r_{13}, r_{14}\}$ as the answers to the window query (with the associated verification objects).

Similarly, the figure also shows a range query $[p_c, r]$ whose correct answers are $\{r_5, r_8, r_9\}$. Here, an adversary may choose to return $\{r_5, r_9\}$ (i.e., an incomplete answer). As another example, the figure also illustrates a 3NN query (i.e., $k = 3$) centered at p_c. The correct answers for this 3NN query are $\{r_5, r_8, r_9\}$. Now, a compromised publisher may return $\{r_4, r_8, r_9\}$ (i.e., an incorrect answer). Likewise, the RNN of r_{14} is $\{r_{13}, r_{15}\}$, and an adversary may simply return $\{r_{13}\}$ (i.e., an incomplete answer). Here, to achieve minimality, the authentication mechanism should ideally return exactly the answers $\{r_5, r_8, r_9\}$ for the range and 3NN queries, and $\{r_{13}, r_{15}\}$ for RNN(r_{14}).

4.2   AUTHENTICATING WINDOW QUERY

A straightforward solution to verify the correction of a window query is to store a multi-dimensional point $(x_{i1}, x_{i2}, \ldots, x_{id})$ in some preferred order, say $x_{i1}|x_{i2}|...|key_{id}$ [Devanbu et al., 2003]. In this way, any existing single dimensional schemes (e.g., those developed for handling relational DBMS queries) can be readily employed. However, such a scheme is expected to be very inefficient for symmetric queries, which are typical in multi-dimensional context. Moreover, it will not preserve the minimality property.

In this section, we shall look at existing methods that are based on spatial partitioning [Cheng and Tan, 2007, 2009, Cheng et al., 2006, Yang et al., 2009] where the multi-dimensional space is split into partitions. Now, to ensure that the answer for a window query is complete, the user must be able to verify that

- All *candidate* partitions that overlap with the query window are examined; and

- All points within each candidate partition that satisfy the query are returned as answers.

Existing methods addressed these issues based on an integration of spatial data structures, Merkle Hash Tree and/or signature chains.

4.2.1   MERKLE HASH-BASED SCHEMES

Under the Merkle hash-based schemes [Yang et al., 2009], all points within a partition is returned, and the Merkle hash tree mechanism is adapted to ensure that no candidate partitions are left out by the server.

The Merkle Hash-based R-tree (MR-tree) [Yang et al., 2009] is an R*-tree structure [Beckmann et al., 1990] embedded with hash values derived in a manner similar to the way a Merkle hash tree is constructed. Figure 4.2(a) shows the partitioning of the data space for our running example under R-tree. The corresponding MR-tree is shown in Figure 4.2(b). The leaf nodes store the data points. The internal nodes store entries of the form (p_i, MBR_i, H_i) where p_i is a pointer to the ith child, MBR_i is the minimum bounding box of the ith child, and H_i is the digest of the ith child. For internal nodes that are immediately above the leaf nodes, the digest is given by a one-way hash function on the concatenation of the data points. For other internal nodes, the digest is derived from both the bounding boxes and digests of the child entries. Figure 4.2(b) shows the entries N_1 (level immediately above leaf nodes) and N_7 (other levels) and the derivation of their digests respectively. We note that the root's digest H is further signed by the data owner and is kept with the tree.

Window queries are processed in a similar manner as it would have been done in a R*-tree. However, besides returning the answer points to a query, verification objects are also attached. For the MR-tree, the verification objects include all points in the leaf nodes whose bounding boxes overlap with the query window as well as the bounding boxes and digests of nodes along the search traversal paths. The signed root digest H_{sign}, must also be returned to the user. With these information, the user will be able to verify the completeness of the query by ensuring that: (a) from the bounding boxes, the user can determine all overlapping regions have been examined; and (b) from the verification objects, the user can recompute the root digest that agrees with H_{sign}.

As an example, consider the window query Q_w in our running example. Besides $\{r_{13}, r_{14}\}$ (which is the answer), the verification object contains $\{r_{15}, r_{19}\}$, (R_4, H_4) of entry N_4, (R_6, H_6) of entry N_6, and (R_7, H_7) of N_7. From the bounding boxes, it is clear that only R_8 and R_5 need to be examined. From the data points $\{r_{13}, r_{14}, r_{15}, r_{19}\}$, the user compute the digest of the corresponding minimum bounding box (which is H_5 in our case); (R_5, H_5) can then be combined with (R_4, H_4) and

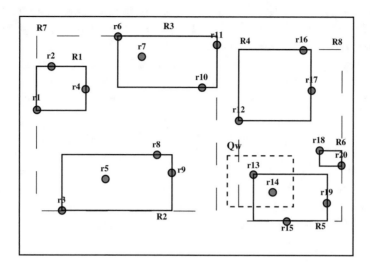

(a) R-tree partitioning

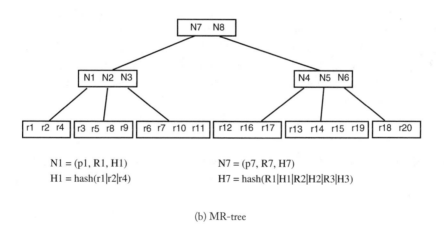

$$N1 = (p1, R1, H1)$$
$$H1 = hash(r1|r2|r4)$$

$$N7 = (p7, R7, H7)$$
$$H7 = hash(R1|H1|R2|H2|R3|H3)$$

(b) MR-tree

Figure 4.2: The MR-tree.

(R_6, H_6) to derive (R_8, H_8); and the root digest, H, can be computed from (R_7, H_7) and (R_8, H_8). Finally, the answer is complete if H is the same as the digest obtained from H_{sign}. In this example, it is.

The correctness of this scheme is based on the assumption that one-way hash functions are collision-resistant. In other words, any form of tampering of the data points will lead to H not being in agreement with H_{sign}. Likewise, if any answers are not returned (e.g., intentionally pruned away by the server), H will not match H_{sign}. Thus, as long as H is equal to the digest obtained from H_{sign}, it can be concluded that the answers are correct.

There are two key limitations with this scheme. First, it is not minimal, i.e., it exposes some other data points that are not answers (e.g., $\{r_{15}, r_{19}\}$). Second, since more data points are returned, the overhead of the verification objects can be very bad. To mitigate these limitation, Yang et al. [2009] extended the MR-tree to further reduce (but not totally remove) the number of non-answer points returned. The resultant tree, MR*-tree, embeds a KD-tree in each leaf node and a box-KD-tree [Agarwal et al., 2002] in each internal node. The basic idea is to partition the space within a node into sub-partitions. In this way, only points in overlapping sub-partitions need to be returned. MR*-tree achieves the same storage requirement as the MR-tree by not materializing a (box) KD-tree. Instead, the data are stored in an order given by an in-order traversal of (box) KD-tree. At runtime, the (box) KD-tree is reconstructed incurring higher CPU cost.

4.2.2   SIGNATURE-CHAIN BASED SCHEMES

Under the signature-chain based schemes [Cheng and Tan, 2009, Cheng et al., 2006], to guarantee correctness and completeness of answers, points within a partition are "connected" using the signature chain concept [Pang et al., 2005]. In this way, only certain points along the chain (and not all points in a partition) need to be returned. In addition, to ensure no candidate partitions has been left out, different methods can be used to certify that all candidate partitions have been examined. Under the *space partitioning* schemes, this can be easily done by verifying that the union of the space covered by the candidate partitions must enclose the query region. For *data partitioning* schemes, chaining has been applied on partitions. Figure 4.3 illustrates this chaining concept for multi-dimensional data using our running example.

Chaining within a partition

To chain points within a partition, they must be first ordered. In Cheng et al. [2006] and Cheng and Tan [2009], points are ordered based on increasing $(x_1, x_2, \ldots, x_d)$ value. In 2-d space, (x_1, y_1) is ordered before (x_2, y_2) if $x_1 < x_2$, or $x_1 = x_2$ and $y_1 < y_2$. As an example, in Figure 4.3(b), the points in partition R2 are ordered (indicated by the arrow in figure) as r_3, r_5, r_8, r_9, while those in partition R3 are ordered as r_6, r_7, r_{10}, r_{11}. This simple scheme is adequate as compared to more sophisticated space filling curves ([Sagan, 1994]) because the number of points within a partition (4K-8K page) is typically small (100-200).

The signature chain for multi-dimensional points is constructed based on this ordering, and generalizes the approach for single-dimensional space [Pang et al., 2005]. In other words, the signature of each point is obtained from its own digest as well as its left and right neighbors' (based on the ordering function) digests. Consider a partition P bounded by two points $p_0 = (x_{01}, x_{02}, \ldots, x_{0d})$ and $p_{k+1} = (x_{(k+1),1}, x_{(k+1),2}, \ldots, x_{(k+1),d})$ where $x_{0r} \leq x_{(k+1),r}$ for all r. Suppose P contains k data points $p_1 = (x_{11}, x_{12}, \ldots, x_{1d}), \ldots p_k = (x_{k1}, x_{k2}, \ldots, x_{kd})$. Further, let us assume that p_i is

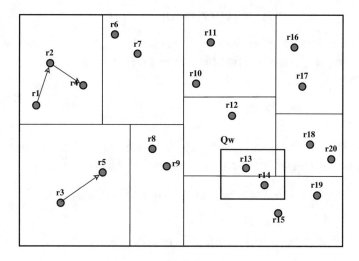

(a) Space partitioning

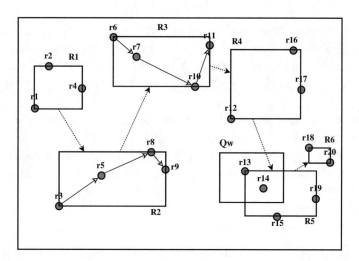

(b) Data partitioning

Figure 4.3: Chaining in multi-dimensional space.

ordered before p_j for $1 \le i < j \le k$. Clearly, p_0 is ordered before p_1 and p_{k+1} is ordered after p_k. Then, point p_i within P has a signature obtained as follows:

$$sig(p_i) = s(\mathcal{H}(g(p_{i-1})|g(p_i)|g(p_{i+1}))) ,$$

where s is a signature function using the owner's private key, $\mathcal{H}$ is a one-way hash function, and $|$ denotes concatenation. $g(p_i)$ is a function to produce a digest for point p_i:

$$g(p_i) = \sum_{r=1}^{d} \mathcal{H}^{U_r - x_{ir} - 1}(x_{ir}) \mid \mathcal{H}^{x_{ir} - L_r - 1}(x_{ir}) , \tag{4.1}$$

where $\mathcal{H}^j(x_{ir}) = \mathcal{H}^{j-1}(\mathcal{H}(x_{ir}))$ and $\mathcal{H}^0(x_{ir})$ applies a one-way hash function on x.

Moreover, for the two delimiters, their signatures are derived as follows:

$$sig(p_0) = s(\mathcal{H}(\mathcal{H}(L_1|\dots|L_d)|g(p_0)|g(p_1)))$$

$$sig(p_{k+1}) = s(\mathcal{H}(g(p_k)|g(p_{k+1})|\mathcal{H}(U_1|\dots|U_d))) .$$

In addition, each partition P has an associated signature:

$$sig(P) = s(\mathcal{H}(g(p_0)|g(p_{k+1})|\mathcal{H}(k))) .$$

Consider a window query $Q = [q_l, q_u]$ where $q_l = (q_{l1}, q_{l2}, \dots, q_{ld})$ and $q_u = (q_{u1}, q_{u2}, \dots, q_{ud})]$. For each partition P that overlaps the Q, the server returns the verification objects that contains: (i) the answer points and their corresponding signatures; (ii) the delimiting points of P and their corresponding signatures; and (iii) the number of points within P, and the signature of P.

In addition, for certain selected non-answer points (i.e., non-answer points along the chain or are boundaries of the chain), their partially computed digests are returned. Specifically, let $\mathcal{F} = \{p_i \in P \mid x_{i1} \in [q_{l1}, q_{u1}] \wedge \exists r \; x_{ir} \notin [q_{lr}, q_{ur}]\}$. Then for each point $p_i \in \mathcal{F} \cup$ {bounding points of the chain}, the server returns partial digests computed as follows: (i) if $x_{ir} \in [q_{lr}, q_{ur}]$, $\mathcal{H}^{U_r - x_{ir} - 1}(x_{ir})|\mathcal{H}^{x_{ir} - L_r - 1}(x_{ir})$ is returned; (ii) if $x_{ir} < q_{lr}$, $\mathcal{H}^{q_{ur} - x_{ir} - 1}(x_{ir})$ and $\mathcal{H}^{x_{ir} - L_r - 1}(x_{ir})$ are returned; (iii) if $x_{ir} > q_{ur}$, $\mathcal{H}^{U_r - x_{ir} - 1}(x_{ir})$ and $\mathcal{H}^{x_{ir} - q_{lr} - 1}(x_{ir})$ are returned. From the partial digests, $g(p_i)$ can be computed without knowing the actual value of p_i.

- If $x_{ir} < q_{lr}$, the user applies $\mathcal{H}$ on $(\mathcal{H}^{q_{ur} - x_{ir} - 1}(x_{ir}))$ $(U_r - q_{ur})$ times to get $(\mathcal{H}^{U_r - x_{ir} - 1}(x_{ir}))$.

- If $x_{ir} > q_{ur}$, the user applies $\mathcal{H}$ on $(\mathcal{H}^{x_{ir} - q_{lr} - 1}(x_{ir}))$ $(q_{lr} - L_r)$ times to get $(\mathcal{H}^{x_{ir} - L_r - 1}(x_{ir}))$.

- The user computes $g(p_i)$ using Equation (4.1).

In this way, partially computed digests offer a mechanism to guarantee minimality as non-answer points are not returned in the plain. These information will then be used to facilitate authenticity and completeness of answers within P.

For example, consider the window query Q_w (see Figure 4.2(a)). In this example, partition R_5 overlaps Q_w. The verification objects are: (i) r_{13}, r_{14}, $sig(r_{13})$, $sig(r_{14})$; (ii) p_0, p_{k+1}, $sig(p_0)$, $sig(p_{k+1})$; (iii) $k = 4$, $sig(R_5)$; and (iv) partially computed digests of r_{15} (its x-value is bounded by the x-values of Q_w), p_0 and r_{19} (bounding points of the chain; p_0 is a bounding point since r_{13} is the left most data answer point).

Now, with the partially computed digests, we can easily determine $g(r_{15})$, $g(r_{19})$, and $g(p_0)$. Next, the user can easily verify that the bounding box is correct by determining whether $s^{-1}(sig(P)) = \mathcal{H}(g(p_0)|g(p_{k+1})|\mathcal{H}(k))$. Then, it can be verified that each answer point (i.e., r_{13} and r_{14}) is in P by checking that p is bounded by P (the bounding box is given by p_0 and p_{k+1}. Finally, it can be verified that r_{13} is authentic by checking that $s^{-1}(sig(r_{13})) = \mathcal{H}(g(p_0)|g(p_{r_{13}})|g(r_{14}))$. Similarly, we can check that r_{14} is authentic. We note that any attempt by the publisher server to cheat would lead to an unsuccessful match in at least one of the above cases. Moreover, since the set of points returned is a superset of the answers, and they are chained, dropping a point will result in an invalid signature for its neighbors (hence we achieve completeness). However, only answer points are returned in the plain, while non-answer points are returned in the form of digests for proving completeness. Thus, only the existence of the data points are revealed, but not their actual content. We note that if a non-answer has the same coordinate as an answer point along some dimension, both points will have the same digest for that dimension and hence the coordinates of those dimensions will be revealed. This can be overcome by introducing some randomness into the hashing function.

Verifying all candidate partitions are covered

Next, let us look at how a user can verify that the query answer covers all the candidate partitions. Essentially, there are two categories of methods. The first category is based on *space* partitioning, while the second category is based on *data* partitioning.

With space partitioning schemes, the partitions are disjoint but their union covers the entire data space. Under such an approach, the verification process turns out to be very straightforward - check that the bounding boxes of the returned partitions are correct, and that the union of these partitions covers the query scope. The former has already been addressed in the previous section, while the latter is just a simple check on the partition boundaries.

To illustrate, Figure 4.3(a) shows the data space being partitioned through a KD-tree In the figure, the window of the query Q_w overlaps three partitions, so only data from these three partitions are returned in the answer. We note that, besides the KD-tree, other spatial indexing techniques like the grid file [Nievergelt et al., 1984] and quadtree [Samet, 1984] can also be employed to help the publisher to locate the candidate partitions quickly. A key advantage with the space partitioning scheme is that the authentication mechanism entails no changes to the spatial data structures (except for the content at the leaf nodes).

With data partitioning approach, the partitions are clusters of data points. However, the union of all the partitions may not cover the entire data space. This poses a challenge to verifying the completeness of query answers: since the space that contains no data points may not be covered by any partition, how can the user be sure that all candidate partitions have been covered while those regions of a query window that are not covered by any returned partitions indeed are empty spaces? Figure 4.3(b) is an example of a data partitioning scheme based on R-tree where only partitions R_1 to R_6 contain data, and other part of the data space contain no data. From Figure 4.3(b), we note that Q_w intersects box R_5 as well as part of the empty space not covered by any data partitions.

The solution proposed by Cheng et al. [2006] essentially extends the signature chain concept to the partitions. Specifically, the partitions are ordered by their starting boundaries along a selected dimension (as is done for point data), and can then be chained such that the signature of a partition is dependent on the neighboring partitions to its left and right. Referring to Figure 4.3(b), the partitions are ordered based on the x-axis of the lower left corner point (see the dashed arrows) as follows: R_1, R_2, R_3, R_4, R_5, R_6.

Let the bounding box of the ith partition be demarcated by $[l, u]$ where $l = (l_{i1}, l_{i2}, \ldots, l_{id})$, and $u = (u_{i1}, u_{i2}, \ldots, u_{id})$. Each partition P_i has an associated signature (based on signature chaining):

$$sig(P_i) = s(\mathcal{H}(g(P_{i-1})|g(P_i)|g(P_{i+1}))) \,,$$

where P_{i-1} and P_{i+1} are the left and right sibling partitions of P_i, and $g(P_i)$ is defined as follows:

$$g(P_i) = \mathcal{H}(\mathcal{H}(l_{i1}|\ldots|l_{id})|\mathcal{H}(u_{i1}|\ldots|u_{id})|\mathcal{H}(k_i)) \,,$$

where k_i is the number of points within P_i. In addition, like the way the signature chain for data points is constructed, two additional fictitious partitions need to be defined as delimiters.

During query processing, all the relevant partition information along with their signatures are returned as part of the query answer. The user can be certain that no partition is omitted, otherwise some signatures will not match. For those partitions that overlap the query window, the user then proceeds to check their data points using the mechanism described earlier. The remaining partitions that do not intersect the query window are dropped from further consideration. Using the window query, Q_w, in Figure 4.3(b), partitions R_3, R_4, R_5 and R_6 are the relevant partitions, while it is clear that partitions R_1, R_2 and R_3 do not need to be considered (and hence are pruned away).

To further minimize the extra partitions that are disclosed to the user, and to reduce performance overheads, a hierarchical data partitioning indexing structure like the R-tree, can be constructed on the data [Cheng et al., 2006]. The partitions within each internal node of the R-tree are chained as described above. Given a window query, the publisher server iteratively expands the child nodes corresponding to those candidate partitions in the current node, starting from the root down to the leaf nodes. All the partition information and signatures along the path of traversal are added to the query answer for user verification.

4.3   AUTHENTICATING KNN/RANGE QUERY

In this section, we look at how kNN/range queries can be authenticated. As a range query $[P_c, r]$ (i.e., query centered at P_c with radius r) can be easily handled in the same way as a kNN query, we shall just focus on verification methods for kNN queries. However, we should add that the actual processing of range queries can be done more efficiently at the publisher since finding points in a hyper-sphere is more straightforward than finding the kNN of a point.

For kNN queries, the methods for window queries can be applied in a straightforward manner. Consider a kNN query $Q_k = [p_c, k]$. The following processing steps are performed.

- The publisher processes Q_k. Let d be the distance between p_c and the kth answer point.

- The publisher creates a window query centered at p_c and whose sides are of length d. In other words, the window query $Q_w = [q_l, q_u]$ where $q_l = (p_{c1} - d, p_{c2} - d, ...p_{cn} - d)$ and $q_u = (p_{c1} + d, p_{c2} + d, ...p_{cn} + d)$ and p_{ci} is the value of the ith dimension of p_c.

- The publisher processes Q_w, and returns the answers in the plain, together with the corresponding verification objects.

- The user receives the answers to Q_k. To verify that these answers are complete and authentic, the user verifies that the answers to Q_w is complete and authentic. Since the answers to Q_w is a superset of the answers to Q_k, the user is assured that the answers to Q_k is complete and authentic.

Using our running example, consider a 3NN query centered at P_c in Figure 4.4. Based on the window-based method, the points $\{r_4, r_5, r_8, r_9\}$ will be returned in the plain, from which the users can further confirm that the answers to the 3NN query are just $\{r_5, r_8, r_9\}$. While this method is simple, it exposes non-answer points in the plain, like r_4 in our example, to users. Unfortunately, the number of such points is not bounded, and can, in the worst case, be very large, e.g., when the non-overlapping regions of the space between Q_w and Q_k is dense. We will next look at a solution that bounds the number of such non-answer points, and another solution where only answer points are returned in the plain.

4.3.1   A COMPUTATIONAL GEOMETRY APPROACH

Hu et al. [2010] proposed the VN-Auth (Voronoi Neighbor Authentication) scheme. Under this scheme, each object in the dataset is associated with a set of *voronoi neighbors* - two objects are voronoi neighbors if they are connected when we construct the `Delaunay triangulation` of the objects in the dataset. Referring to our example in Figure 4.4(a), the neighbors of $r_8 = \{r_4, r_5, r_7, r_9, r_{10}, r_{12}\}$. The outsourced dataset consists of triples of the form for each object o: $(o, o_{neighbors}, o_{sig})$ where $o_{neighbors}$ contains the neighbors of o, and o_{sig} is o's signature computed from a concatenation of o and $o_{neighbors}$. The dataset can then be indexed at the publisher using any spatial indexing structures.

For a kNN query, the publisher processes it using its own algorithm (based on its own index structure), and returns: (a) the k answer objects; (b) an aggregated signature obtained from combining the signatures of answer objects [Mykletun et al., 2004, 2006]; and (c) for each answer object, its voronoi neighbors. With these k answer objects, the user can easily recompute the aggregated signature to verify the answers have not been tampered with.

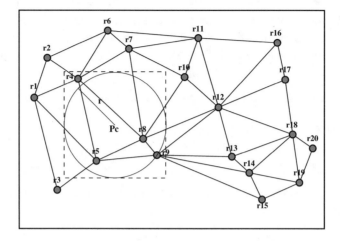

(a) Delaunay triangulation

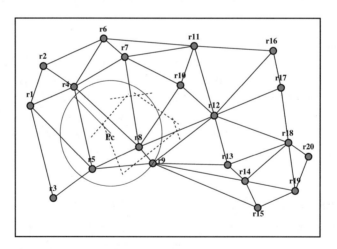

(b) VN-Auth

Figure 4.4: Authenticating kNN queries.

To verify that the answers are complete, properties of voronoi diagrams are exploited—essentially, a point p is a 1st NN of a query point q if p and q are in the same voronoi cell; the 2nd NN of q is one of p's voronoi neighbors; and the kth NN of q is one of the vornonoi neighbors of the $(k-1)$ NNs of q. Let the k NNs be $\{p_1, p_2, \ldots, p_k\}$ where p_i is the ith NN of q. The verification process works as follows. First, the voronoi cell of p_1 is constructed from its

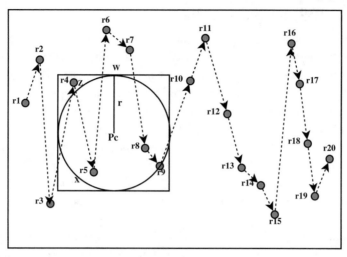

Figure 4.5: Hiding non-answer points in kNN queries.

voronoi neighbors. With this, it is easy to verify that p_1 is indeed the 1st NN. Next, from the voronoi neighbors of p_1, the one closest to q, say p, should be p_2. This verification process of: (a) obtaining the union of the voronoi neighbors of the verified answer objects, say U; (b) finding the object in U that is nearest to q; and (c) comparing against the next NN to be verified, is repeated until all the answer objects are verified. At any instance where the verification process fails, it means the answers are incomplete.

Let's illustrate the verification process using our running example in Figure 4.4(b). Here, we have a 3NN query centered at P_c. The publisher returns r_8 as the 1st NN, r_5 as the 2nd NN, and r_9 as the 3rd NN. From the neighbors of r_8, the voronoi cell is constructed, and it is verified that r_8 is indeed the 1st NN. From r_8's neighbors, it is clear that r_5 is the one closest to P_c, and so confirming that r_5 is a valid answer point. Finally, from the neighbors of r_8 and r_5, we have r_0 being nearest to P_c.

The VN-Auth scheme has several advantages. In particular, the data owner and the publisher operate independently, i.e., the publisher can adopt any indexing structures and processing mechanisms. This is in contrast to schemes that are based on Merkle hash structures. Moreover, any updates only affect a small local region (the neighborhood of the affected points). In addition, for each object, the average number of neighbors is at most six (though the worst case may be larger) which implies that the number of non-answer points that are returned in the plain is at most (on average) $6 \times |answers|$.

4.3.2   A SIGNATURE-BASED SCHEME

So far, all the schemes for processing kNN queries that we have encountered cannot guarantee minimality. While the signature-based scheme offers minimality guarantee for window queries, it cannot be directly applied for kNN queries. As an example, consider a 2NN query centered at P_c in Figure 4.5. Suppose the adversary returns r_5 and r_9 in the plain together with the digests for r_3, r_4, r_6, r_7, r_8 and r_{10}. Clearly, the signature chain can be verified to be correct. However, it cannot be determined that answer points may have been dropped. In fact, in our example, r_8 has been dropped. The verification scheme for window queries cannot be applied because there is no way to tell from the digest of r_8 whether it is enclosed by the bounding hyper-sphere of the 2NN answers (in which case we can be sure an answer has been dropped), or it falls just outside of the hyper-sphere (e.g., like r_4) but within the MBR that bounds the hyper-sphere (in which case we can be sure it is not an answer point).

To ensure minimality, Cheng and Tan [2007, 2009] built on and extended the signature-based scheme to enable digests of non-answer points to be computed collaboratively between the user and the publisher. The scheme, called *collaborative digest computation*, works as follows. For each non-answer point p whose digest is to be used for verification, instead of returning the digest of p, the publisher returns $(\tilde{p}, q)$-pair to the user where $\tilde{p}$ is a partial computation of the digest of p with reference to q. The user can then determine the digest of p from $\tilde{p}$ and q. Moreover, by picking q that is outside of the answer region, the user can determine that p is not part of the answers.

Formally, let p and q be two points $p = \{x_1, x_2, ..., x_d\}, q = \{y_1, y_2, ..., y_d\}$, such that $x_i < y_i$ $\forall i$. Recall that the one-way hash function g (Equation 4.1) used to compute the digest of a point is an iterative hash function. Then, instead of returning the digest of p directly, the server can compute $\mathcal{H}^{y_i - x_i - 1}(x_i)$ and $\mathcal{H}^{x_i - L_i - 1}(x_i)$. The user will then derive $g(p)$ using Equation 4.1 after applying $\mathcal{H}$ on $(\mathcal{H}^{y_i - x_i - 1}(x_i))$ an additional of $(U_i - y_i)$ times to get $(\mathcal{H}^{U_i - x_i - 1}(x_i)) \forall i$. Now, similar computation can be derived for different relations between x_i and y_i. Thus, we can determine the digest of p collaboratively without revealing p.

Returning to our 2NN example in Figure 4.5, with collaborative digest computation, the publisher will not be able to find a point q outside of the hyper-sphere for which the digest of r_8 can be computed correctly. On the other hand, for r_4, the reference point can be the point at location Z, and it is clear that r_4 is outside of the hyper-sphere as Z is outside (otherwise, the digest of r_4 cannot be computed).

Putting all these together, the resultant scheme to verify answers of kNN queries works as follows [Cheng and Tan, 2007]. Let $[p_c, k]$ be a kNN query centered at p_c. Once the publisher computes the k answers, it returns only the k answers in plaintext. In addition, it also returns the following verification objects.

- It returns the k signatures of the answer points. These are used to verify that the data have not been tampered with.

- The k points returned may not fall into a consecutive sequence along the signature chain. For example, in Figure 4.1, there is a gap between r_5 and r_8 (i.e., there are points between r_5 and r_8 which are not answer points). Thus, the publisher will also need to return the partial computation of the digests of a number of points that form a chain. Referring to our example again, the partial digests of points r_3, r_4, r_6, r_7 and r_{10} need to be returned. Here, the digest of r_3 is also returned in order to be certain that there is no point within the hyper-sphere that is chained between r_3 and r_4. The user will then derive the digests of these points to verify the authenticity of the answer points. For example, by computing the digests of r_4 and r_6, the authenticity of r_5 can be verified. Similarly, with the digest of r_7, r_8 can be verified to be authentic. Similarly, the digest of r_{10} is needed to verify the authenticity of r_9.

- Now, to verify that the answers are indeed the k answer points, the user needs to show that all other points in the chain are outside of the hyper-sphere centered at P_c with radius r, where $r = dist(P_c, kth\ answer\ point)$. Using our example, the user needs to verify that r_3, r_4, r_6, r_7 and r_{10} are outside of the hyper-sphere. To do this, the publisher also returns a set of reference points. Let the number of non-answer points returned be M. Then, the number of reference points needed is (at most) M, one for each of the non-answer points. These reference points are points in the space but not from the dataset. Moreover, they are points on or outside of the hyper-sphere surface so that the distance between these points and P_c is larger than or equal to r, but shorter than the distance between their corresponding non-answer points and P_c. Note that the publisher can easily determine these points since it knows all the points in the dataset. Using our running example again, r_3 has a reference point X, r_4 has a reference point Z, and r_6 and r_7 have the same reference point W. For each (non-answer point, reference point) pair, the partial digest of the non-answer point is computed by the publisher (as described earlier), and the user can complete the computation and derive the actual digest of the non-answer point. As long as the digest is valid, the user will know that the non-answer point is outside of the hyper-sphere (since it knows that the distance between P_c and the reference point is larger than the radius of the hyper-sphere).

Considering our running example in Figure 4.5 again, let us consider the 3NN query centered at P_c. The answers, $\{r_5, r_8, r_9\}$, are returned in plaintext. In addition, the publisher also returns: (a) the signatures of the 3 answer points, which are $sig(r_5)$, $sig(r_8)$ and $sig(r_9)$; (b) two pairs $(\tilde{r}_3, B_1)$ and $(\tilde{r}_{10}, B_2)$, where $\tilde{r}_3$ and $\tilde{r}_{10}$ are the partial computation of the digests of r_3 and r_{10} respectively. These are for the two boundary points r_3 and r_{10} of the answer's signature chain. Points B_1 and B_2 are the leftmost and rightmost point of the hyper-sphere query respectively, where $B_1.x = P_c.x - dist(P_c, r_9)$ and $B_2.x = P_c.x + dist(P_c, r_9)$; and (c) pairs $(\tilde{r}_4, Z)$, $(\tilde{r}_6, W)$, and $(\tilde{r}_7, W)$ respectively, where $\tilde{r}_i$ is the partial digest of point r_i, Z and W are the corresponding reference points selected for each r_i. These are for points r_4, r_6, and r_7 that fall into the gap of the answer points along the consecutive signature chain sequence. With all these information, the user can verify the authenticity and completeness of the answers with minimality guarantee.

Like the window queries, data structures can be developed to improve performance so that only the necessary portion of the dataset needs to be examined. In particular, R*-tree [Beckmann et al., 1990] and iDistance [Yu et al., 2001] based-schemes were designed [Cheng and Tan, 2007]. The idea is to partition the space recursively and partitions of a level are signature chained as well as points within a partition are signature chained. The processing logic follows that of the schemes for verifying window queries: as the data structure is traversed, it has to be ensured that no partitions and points are missed out based on the chaining of the partitions and points.

4.4   AUTHENTICATING REVERSE NEAREST NEIGHBOR QUERIES

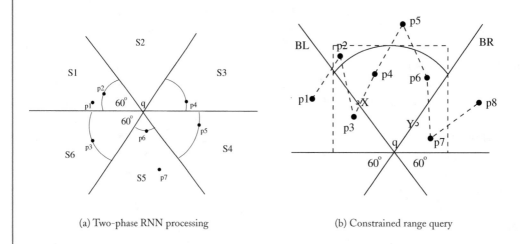

(a) Two-phase RNN processing   (b) Constrained range query

Figure 4.6: RNN query processing.

A two-phase algorithm has been proposed [Ferhatosmanoglu et al., 2001] to retrieve the RNN of a query point q in a 2-dimensional data space. In the first phase, the data space around the query point q is divided into six equal regions S_1 to S_6. For each region S_i ($1 \leq i \leq 6$), a constrained NN query (i.e., a NN query restricted to a region only) is processed to retrieve the nearest neighbors of q in that region. Let the point for S_i be p_i. It turns out that these six points constitute the candidate result set. In other words, either $p_i \in RNN(q)$ or (ii) there is no RNN of q in S_i. Thus, in the second phase, a NN query is applied to find the NN of each candidate p_i. We denote the NN of p_i as p_i'. If $dist(p_i, q) < dist(p_i, p_i')$, then p_i belongs to the actual result; otherwise, it is a false hit and discarded.

As an example, consider Figure 4.6 which divides the 2-dimensional space around a query point q into six equal regions S_1 to S_6. In Figure 4.6, the NN of q in S_1 is point p_2. However, the NN of p_2 is p_1. Consequently, there is no RNN of q in S_1 and we do not need to search further in this region. The same is true for S_2 (no data points), S_3, S_4 (p_4, p_5 are NNs of each other) and S_6 (the NN of p_3 is p_1). There is only one answer for RNN(q) which is p_6 in region S_5.

Now, since both phases of the above scheme consist of a series of NN queries, the kNN authentication scheme can be applied. We shall discuss the signature-based authentication scheme proposed by Cheng and Tan [2009] that guarantees authentication, completeness and minimality. The scheme is based on the collaborative digest computation discussed earlier. Before we present the scheme, let us review this concept in the context of a constrained range query using Figure 4.4(b) as an example. Here, the data space is split into 6 equal regions. A constrained range query centered at q and radius r is one that is restricted to one region (e.g., the region bounded by the two lines BL and BR). As we have seen, such a query is useful when we process RNN queries. For a constrained range query, certain points can be hidden in a similar way window queries (e.g., p_1, p_5 and p_8) and range/kNN queries (e.g., p_2) are handled. For points like p_3 and p_7, the same concept of reference points can still be used. In our example, for p_3, a reference point X on the line BL can be picked. Note that the user needs to verify that the reference point is on the line BL. Now, we can use the collaborative approach for the user to compute the digest of p_3. Using the same logic, a reference point Y can be used to facilitate the collaborative computation of the digest of p_7 without returning p_7 in the plain.

The authentication scheme comprises two cases: (a) the point p_i in region S_i is indeed the RNN of q; and (b) the point p_i in region S_i is not the RNN of q. Note that for case (b), both p_i as well as its NN have to be hidden in order to show that its NN is not q.

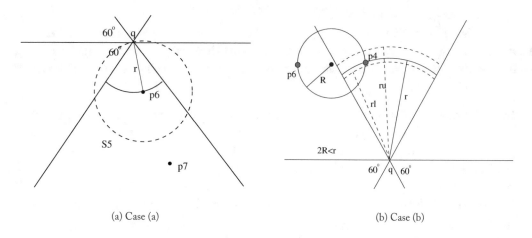

(a) Case (a)   (b) Case (b)

Figure 4.7: Authenticating RNN queries.

Case (a): p_i **in region** S_i **is the RNN of** q

When the publisher returns p_i in region S_i as the answer (in the plain), the user needs to do the following to verify that it is indeed an answer (we also describe the verification objects that the publisher need to return).

- Verify that p_i is the NN of q. To do this, the publisher returns the results of the constrained range query with q as the center and $r = dist(p_i, q)$ as the radius. A constrained range query refers to the query being bounded by the splitting plane of the region. Here, the results consist of p_i, the partial digests of points that are along the signature chain, and the associated reference points. With these information, it can be verified if p_i is indeed the only point, and if so, it is the NN of q. Otherwise, it means that the publisher has cheated.

- Verify that q is the NN of p_i. To do this, the publisher returns the results of a range query centered at p_i with radius r (together with the associated signature chain, and reference points). Clearly, as long as there is no answer point for this query (q is a query point), it means that q is the NN of p_i. Thus, it can be concluded that p_i is a RNN of q.

Figure 4.7(a) illustrates an example. Here, region S_5 has two points p_6 and p_7. Since p_6 is the answer, it will be returned in the plain. From the first constrained range query centered at q with radius $r = dist(q, p_6)$, it can be determined that p_6 is indeed the NN of q. The second range query centered at p_6 with radius r would confirm that no points are within this query region, and hence p_6 is the correct answer. From the figure, it is clear that p_7 is further away to p_6 than q.

Case (b): p_i **in region** S_i **is not the RNN of** q

In this case, since p_i is not an RNN of q, p_i cannot be returned in the plain. However, there is a need to (1) verify that p_i is an NN of q, and (2) verify that there exists another point t such that $dist(p_i, t) < dist(p_i, q)$. Note that these have to be done without revealing p_i and t. This can be done as follows.

- It can be observed that two reference points are sufficient to verify that a point (without revealing it in the plain) is in a query region. Thus, the publisher returns two reference points X and Y such that: (a) $r_l = dist(q, X) < r_u = dist(q, Y)$; (b) p_i is the only answer of a constrained range query centered at q with radius r_u; (c) there are no answer points of a constrained range query centered at q with radius r_l. Now, since the user knows X and Y, he/she can easily verify that no points are in the constrained range query $[q, r_l]$ and only p_i is in $[q, r_u]$.

- To verify that $dist(p_i, t) < r_l$, the publisher needs to also return a reference point v such that a range query centered at v with radius, R, contains p_i and t. Note that $R \geq dist(p_i, t)/2$. As long as $dist(p_i, t) < 2R < r_l$, the verification succeeds. Thus, the publisher needs to choose 4 additional reference points - 2 to verify that p_i is in the range query, and 2 to verify that t is in the range query. With the four reference points, the publisher is able to determine R.

Figure 4.7(b) illustrates an example. Here, the restricted region has one point p_4 which is the NN of q. However, p_4's NN is p_6. The scheme first finds reference points and r_l and r_u that can be used to verify the boundaries of p_4. Similarly, reference points can be determined so as to find the boundaries that enclose p_6 and p_4. As shown, in this figure, $2R < r_l < r$ and hence it can be determined that p_4 is not an RNN(q) without revealing p_4 and p_6.

4.5   SUMMARY

In this chapter, we presented methods designed for authenticating answers of queries on outsourced spatial databases. A wide variety of query types has been investigated including window, range, kNN and RNN queries. Most of these methods integrate relational authentication mechanisms (e.g., Merkle Hash Tree and signature methods with spatial data structures (e.g., R*-tree, distance).

We believe there is much scope for research on authenticating queries over spatial data. For example, the researches so far focused on static datasets. However, as spatial data such as location data are continuously being collected and used in real-time applications, it becomes very critical to develop techniques that can handle such dynamic and streaming context. Moreover, existing works are restricted to largely the authenticity, completeness and minimality guarantees. In a dynamic context, data freshness is an important criterion. In addition, in such situations, the high frequent updates of data pose a challenge to performance. In particular, schemes that rely on precomputation of static data are no longer applicable. Instead, techniques that are robust to frequent updates are highly desirable. Finally, there is a need to address authentication of more complex queries, e.g., those involving spatial joins, and skylines.

CHAPTER 5

Text Search Queries

Professional users commonly require certain security provisions from their paid content services. This is particularly so in the financial and legal industries. One security provision is *integrity assurance* [Pfleeger and Pfleeger, 2003]—that the content and search results received are correct, and have not been tampered with. For example, a patent examiner using MicroPatent's Web portal would expect from it the same search results as the up-to-date CD-ROM version.

Naturally, the administrator of a search engine would employ a combination of security safeguards, such as firewalls and intrusion detection. Notwithstanding that, servers that are situated in a seemingly well-guarded network can often still be infiltrated. Indeed, the increasing number of successful attacks on online servers over the past decade demonstrates that it is very difficult to guarantee the security of all the servers over extended periods of time. In the event that a search engine is compromised, it could return tampered results.

- *Incomplete results* that omit some legitimate documents. In the MicroPatent case, an attacker could cause his patents to drop out of the search results (to prevent competitors from discovering them), by tampering with the query, the index, or the similarity ranking function.

- *Altered ranking* that deviates from the correct similarity ranking. In the MicroPatent system, for instance, the attacker may divert the searcher's attention from certain patents, or tamper with the document ordering to bias the search results.

- *Spurious results* that include some fake documents. For example, a MicroPatent attacker may seek to discourage potential competitors by adding fake patents to their search results.

In this chapter, we address query answer authentication in text search. We begin by defining the properties that the correct answer for a text search query must possess. Following that, we present the solutions given by Pang and Mouratidis [2008], which map the task of similarity text retrieval to adaptations of two existing threshold-based list merging algorithms.

5.1   BACKGROUND ON TEXT SEARCH

Most text search engines rate the similarity of each document to a query (i.e., a set of keywords) based on these heuristics [Zobel and Moffat, 2006]: (a) terms that appear in many documents are given less weight; (b) terms that appear many times in a document are given more weight; and (c) documents that contain many terms are given less weight. The heuristics are encapsulated in a similarity function, which uses some composition of the following statistical values:

- $f_{d,t}$, the number of times that term t appears in document d;

- $f_{Q,t}$, the number of times that term t appears in query Q;

- f_t, the number of documents that contain term t; and

- n, the number of documents in the data set $\mathcal{D}$.

A similarity function that is effective in practice is the Okapi formulation, which defines the score of a document d with respect to a query Q, $S(d|Q)$, to be:

$$S(d|Q) = \sum_{t \in Q} w_{Q,t} \times w_{d,t} \,, \tag{5.1}$$

where

$$
\begin{aligned}
w_{Q,t} &= \ln\left(\frac{n - f_t + 0.5}{f_t + 0.5}\right) \times f_{Q,t} \\
w_{d,t} &= \frac{(k_1 + 1) f_{d,t}}{K_d + f_{d,t}} \\
K_d &= k_1\left((1 - b) + b\frac{W_d}{W_A}\right) .
\end{aligned}
$$

In the above formulation, k_1 and b are parameters with recommended settings of 1.2 and 0.75 respectively; while W_d and W_A are the document length and average document length. Intuitively, $w_{d,t}$ ($w_{Q,t}$) is the normalized frequency of term t in document d (in query Q, respectively) and represents its significance therein.

Given a query, a straightforward evaluation algorithm is to compute $S(d|Q)$ for each document d in turn, and return those documents with the highest similarity scores at the end. The execution time of this algorithm is proportional to n, which is not scalable to large collections. Instead, search engines make use of an index that maps terms to the documents that contain them. The most efficient index structure for this purpose is the inverted index. In this book, we assume its most recommended variant, the *frequency-ordered inverted index* [Zobel and Moffat, 2006], and describe it below. For brevity, we refer to it simply as inverted index.

Inverted Index. The index consists of two components—a *dictionary* of terms and a set of *inverted lists*. The dictionary stores, for each distinct term t:

- a count f_t of the documents that contain t; and

- a pointer to the head of the corresponding inverted list.

The inverted list for a term t is a sequence of impact entries $\langle d, w_{d,t} \rangle$ where:

- d is the identifier of a document that contains t;

term id	term t	f_t		Inverted List for t
1	and	1	$\mapsto$	$\langle 6, 0.159 \rangle$
2	big	2	$\mapsto$	$\langle 2, 0.148 \rangle \ \langle 3, 0.088 \rangle$
3	dark	1	$\mapsto$	$\langle 6, 0.079 \rangle$
4	did	1	$\mapsto$	$\langle 4, 0.125 \rangle$
5	gown	1	$\mapsto$	$\langle 2, 0.074 \rangle$
6	had	1	$\mapsto$	$\langle 3, 0.088 \rangle$
7	house	2	$\mapsto$	$\langle 3, 0.088 \rangle \ \langle 2, 0.074 \rangle$
8	in	5	$\mapsto$	$\langle 6, 0.159 \rangle \ \langle 2, 0.148 \rangle \ \langle 5, 0.142 \rangle \ \langle 1, 0.058 \rangle \ \langle 7, 0.058 \rangle \ \langle 8, 0.053 \rangle$
				$\ldots$
9	keep	3	$\mapsto$	$\langle 5, 0.088 \rangle \ \langle 1, 0.088 \rangle \ \langle 3, 0.088 \rangle$
10	keeper	3	$\mapsto$	$\langle 4, 0.125 \rangle \ \langle 5, 0.088 \rangle \ \langle 1, 0.088 \rangle$
11	keeps	3	$\mapsto$	$\langle 5, 0.088 \rangle \ \langle 1, 0.088 \rangle \ \langle 6, 0.079 \rangle$
12	light	1	$\mapsto$	$\langle 6, 0.079 \rangle$
13	night	3	$\mapsto$	$\langle 5, 0.177 \rangle \ \langle 4, 0.125 \rangle \ \langle 1, 0.088 \rangle$
14	old	4	$\mapsto$	$\langle 2, 0.148 \rangle \ \langle 4, 0.125 \rangle \ \langle 1, 0.088 \rangle \ \langle 3, 0.088 \rangle$
15	sleeps	1	$\mapsto$	$\langle 6, 0.079 \rangle$
16	the	6	$\mapsto$	$\langle 5, 0.265 \rangle \ \langle 3, 0.263 \rangle \ \langle 6, 0.200 \rangle \ \langle 1, 0.159 \rangle \ \langle 2, 0.148 \rangle \ \langle 4, 0.125 \rangle$
				$\ldots$

Figure 5.1: Example of frequency-ordered inverted list.

- $w_{d,t}$ is the associated frequency of term t in document d, as defined in the context of Formula (5.1).

Each inverted list is sorted in decreasing $w_{d,t}$ order. Figure 5.1 gives an example of a frequency-ordered inverted index, while Figure 5.2 gives the algorithm for evaluating queries with the inverted index, both adapted from [Zobel and Moffat, 2006]. Given a query, the algorithm begins by calculating $w_{Q,t}$ for each query term t, from $f_{Q,t}$ (derived from the term composition of the query) and f_t (stored in the dictionary). The algorithm then repeatedly reads the impact entry with the largest term score $c = w_{Q,t} \times w_{d,t}$ among the inverted lists of the query terms, until all the lists are exhausted. We refer to this algorithm as PSCAN, for Prioritized Scanning.

5.2   PROBLEM FORMULATION

System Model. Our system model involves three parties—the data owner, search engine, and users.

The data owner manages a data collection $\mathcal{D}$ comprising n documents, $\mathcal{D} = \{d_1, d_2, \ldots, d_n\}, n \geq 1$. To provide similarity text searches, the data owner generates an inverted index on $\mathcal{D}$. The index has two parts—a dictionary and a set of inverted lists. Let $\mathcal{T}$ denote the dictionary of search terms for $\mathcal{D}$, $\mathcal{T} = \{t_1, t_2, \ldots, t_m\}, m \geq 1$. The inverted list $\mathcal{L}_i$

To find the top r matching documents for a query $\mathcal{Q}$, using a frequency-ordered inverted index.

---

(1) Fetch the first $\langle d, w_{d,t} \rangle$ entry in each query term t's inverted list.

(2) While inverted list entries remain,

    (a) Identify the inverted list entry $\langle d, w_{d,t} \rangle$ with the highest term score $c = w_{\mathcal{Q},t} \times w_{d,t}$, breaking ties arbitrarily.

    (b) If d has not been encountered before, create an accumulator A_d and initialize it to zero.

    (c) $A_d \leftarrow A_d + c$.

    (d) Fetch the next entry in term t's inverted list.

(3) Identify the r largest A_d values and return the corresponding documents.

Figure 5.2: Prioritized Scanning (PSCAN) Algorithm.

for term $\mathcal{T}.t_i$ is a list of l_i impact pairs, ordered in non-increasing frequency values. Formally, $\mathcal{L}_i = [\langle d_1, f_1 \rangle, \langle d_2, f_2 \rangle, \ldots, \langle d_{l_i}, f_{l_i} \rangle]$ such that: (a) $\forall j \in [1, l_i]$, $\mathcal{L}_i.d_j$ is a document in the collection ($\mathcal{L}_i.d_j \in \mathcal{D}$) and $\mathcal{L}_i.f_j = w_{\mathcal{L}_i.d_j, \mathcal{T}.t_i}$ is $\mathcal{T}.t_i$'s frequency in the document ($w_{d,t}$ is defined in the context of Formula (5.1)); and (b) $\forall j, k$ such that $1 \leq j < k \leq l_i$, $\mathcal{L}_i.f_j \geq \mathcal{L}_i.f_k$. The data owner transfers the document collection, the inverted index, and the query processing software to a third party, which is contracted to operate the search engine.

The search engine accepts natural language text queries from the users. A user query $\mathcal{Q}$ containing q unique search terms is translated to $\mathcal{Q} = \{\langle t_1, f_1 \rangle, \langle t_2, f_2 \rangle, \ldots, \langle t_q, f_q \rangle\}$ such that: (a) the search terms are in the dictionary ($\forall j \in [1, q]$, $\mathcal{Q}.t_j \in \mathcal{T}$); and (b) the frequencies of the terms in $\mathcal{Q}$ are $\mathcal{Q}.f_j = w_{\mathcal{Q}, \mathcal{Q}.t_j}$ $\forall j \in [1, q]$ ($w_{\mathcal{Q}, \mathcal{Q}.t_j}$ is defined in the context of Formula (5.1)). Any query terms that are not in the dictionary are ignored.

The query answer for $\mathcal{Q}$ that is returned to the user, $\mathcal{R}$, is an ordered list of r entries, $\mathcal{R} = [\langle d_1, s_1 \rangle, \langle d_2, s_2 \rangle, \ldots, \langle d_r, s_r \rangle]$, in which $\forall j \in [1, r]$, $\mathcal{R}.d_j \in \mathcal{D}$ are the result documents and $\mathcal{R}.s_j \in \mathbb{R}$ are their corresponding similarity scores.

Correctness of Query Result. A correct query answer $\mathcal{R}$ should relate to query $\mathcal{Q}$ and underlying document collection $\mathcal{D}$ in the following way. We define the frequency of a document d with respect to a query $\mathcal{Q}$, $freq(d|\mathcal{Q})$, to be the vector of frequency values associated with d in the inverted list for each query term. Formally, $freq(d|\mathcal{Q}) = [f_1, f_2, \ldots, f_q]$ where $\forall j \in [1, q]$, $\mathcal{L}_i$ is the inverted list of search term $\mathcal{Q}.t_j$ (i.e., $\mathcal{T}.t_i = \mathcal{Q}.t_j$), and $d.f_j$ satisfies one of the following conditions:

- if d is in $\mathcal{L}_i$, i.e., $\exists k \in [1, l_i]$, $\mathcal{L}_i.d_k = d$, then $d.f_j$ is the frequency associated with d in $\mathcal{L}_i$, i.e., $d.f_j = \mathcal{L}_i.f_k$;

- if d is not in $\mathcal{L}_i$, i.e., $\forall k \in [1, l_i]$, $\mathcal{L}_i.d_k \neq d$, then $d.f_j = 0$.

The similarity score of a document d with respect to a query $\mathcal{Q}$ is $S(d|\mathcal{Q}) = \sum_{j=1}^{q} w_{\mathcal{Q}, \mathcal{Q}.t_j} \times d.f_j = \sum_{j=1}^{q} w_{\mathcal{Q}, \mathcal{Q}.t_j} \times w_{d,t_j}$.

Correctness Criteria: The query result $\mathcal{R}$ is correct if and only if it satisfies the following conditions:

- the result entries are ordered in non-increasing similarity scores, i.e., $\forall j, k$ such that $1 \le j < k \le r$, $\mathcal{R}.s_j \ge \mathcal{R}.s_k$ where $\mathcal{R}.s_j = S(\mathcal{R}.d_j|\mathcal{Q})$ and $\mathcal{R}.s_k = S(\mathcal{R}.d_k|\mathcal{Q})$;

- all the documents that are excluded from $\mathcal{R}$ have lower similarity scores than the last result entry, i.e., for any non-result document $d \in \mathcal{D}$, it holds that $S(d|\mathcal{Q}) \le \mathcal{R}.s_r$.

Threat Model. Among the entities in our system model, the third-party search engine is the potential adversary. The search engine could be subverted by attackers, or the data owner may not be in a position to qualify the administration procedures employed by the contracted third party. In either case, we assume that the search engine may alter the document collection or the inverted index, it may execute the query processing algorithm incorrectly, or it may tamper with the search results. The users therefore need to verify the correctness of the query results.

5.3   CHOICE OF AUTHENTICATION APPROACH

The correctness criteria above hinge on the document scores with respect to the query, $S(d|\mathcal{Q})$. To convince the user that the query result is correct, we therefore need to prove the correctness of the relative document scores. The general approaches include the following.

1. Pre-certify the document scores. This approach was taken by Pang and Tan [2008] in authenticating multi-dimensional range aggregates. As $S(d|\mathcal{Q})$ depends on the query terms as well as on $w_{\mathcal{Q},t}$, it is not feasible to materialize all possible document scores beforehand to support ad-hoc search queries.

2. Certify the frequency $w_{d,t}$ for every combination of document $d \in \mathcal{D}$ and term $t \in \mathcal{T}$. Given a query $\mathcal{Q}$, the search engine returns the $w_{d,t}$ values, along with their signatures, for every $d \in \mathcal{D}$ and $t \in \mathcal{Q}$. After verifying the frequencies, the user then computes $S(d|\mathcal{Q})$ himself to find the top r matching documents. The problem with this approach is that the communication cost (to transmit the $q \times n$ certified frequency values) and the user computation overhead (to verify the frequency values and to generate the query result) are prohibitive, thus rendering the approach impractical.

3. Pre-certify every inverted list, and return to the user those that correspond to the query terms. After checking the integrity of the lists, the user may compute the document scores to produce the query result. This approach fits naturally with the PSCAN algorithm in Figure 5.2. However, the retrieval of entire lists imposes very large I/O costs on the search engine. Also, returning the entire inverted lists as proof incurs excessive communication cost, as well as high verification and memory requirements at the user-side.

4. Dynamically generate certified fragments of the inverted lists. For general ad-hoc queries that are likely to include one or more common terms, it is desirable to return only small fractions of the inverted lists, and still allow the query result to be verified.

Pang and Mouratidis [2008] proposed authenticated threshold algorithms that adopt the last approach. This choice was motivated by the observation that the inverted lists for real corpora follow a highly skewed distribution. Most of the terms have very short inverted lists, whereas a small minority of the inverted lists are several orders of magnitude longer. To illustrate, Figure 5.3 plots the list length distribution for the WSJ corpus, comprising 172,961 articles published in the Wall Street Journal from December 1986 to March 1992. More than 50% of the terms have only between 2 and 5 entries in their inverted lists, whereas the longest list contains 127,848 entries. With such a distribution, most queries are likely to hit one or more short inverted lists, due to their sheer numbers. At the same time, the long lists correspond to the common terms, so they are likely to be queried too. In practice, most queries would involve a mix of long and short inverted lists. For such queries, the short lists are expected to contribute most of the result documents, because they have smaller f_t's and hence larger $w_{Q,t}$ weights compared to the long lists, while only a few leading entries are needed from the long lists. Therefore, it is advantageous to avoid transmitting to the users the long inverted lists in their entirety. In Sections 5.4 and 5.5 we describe two schemes that achieve this objective.

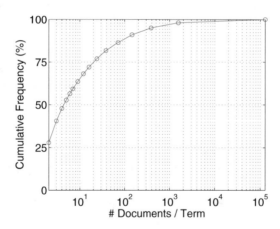

Figure 5.3: Inverted list length distribution for WSJ corpus.

5.4   THRESHOLD WITH RANDOM ACCESS

The first query processing algorithm is Threshold with Random Access (TRA). It modifies the PSCAN algorithm (in Figure 5.2) to terminate once it determines that the inverted lists are not able to produce new documents with a large enough similarity score to qualify for the query result. The TRA algorithm is summarized in Figure 5.4.

To find the top r matching documents for a query Q, using a frequency-ordered inverted index.

---

(1) Initialize the sorted list $\mathcal{R}$.

(2) Fetch the first $\langle d, f \rangle$ entry in each query term t_i's inverted list $\mathcal{L}_i$.

(3) Compute $thres = \sum_{i=1}^{q} w_{Q,Q.t_i} \times \mathcal{L}_i.f$.

(4) While inverted list entries remain,

    (a) If $\mathcal{R}.s_r \geq thres$, go to step (5).

    (b) Pop the inverted list entry $\langle d, f \rangle$ with the highest term score $c_i = w_{Q,Q.t_i} \times \mathcal{L}_i.f$, breaking ties arbitrarily.

    (c) If d has not been encountered before,

        (i) Retrieve w_{d,t_j} for every query term t_j.

        (ii) Compute d's similarity score $s = S(d|Q)$.

        (iii) Insert $\langle d, s \rangle$ into $\mathcal{R}$.

    (d) Update $thres$.

(5) Return the first r entries in $\mathcal{R}$ as the query result.

Figure 5.4: Threshold with Random Access (TRA) Algorithm.

The algorithm repeatedly reads off the next entry $\langle d_j, f_j \rangle$ from the inverted list $\mathcal{L}_i$ with the largest term score $c_i = w_{Q,Q.t_i} \times \mathcal{L}_i.f_j$ among the inverted lists of the query terms. Document $\mathcal{L}_i.d_j$'s similarity score s is immediately computed (hence Random Access) by fetching directly the query term frequencies from the document-MHT (a structure that is additionally used for proof construction and is described shortly). An entry $\langle d, s \rangle$ for this document is then inserted into the result list $\mathcal{R}$, which is ordered by descending s. TRA also maintains a threshold $thres$ that is computed over the current term score c_i of each inverted list, $thres = \sum_{i=1}^{q} c_i$. The threshold forms an upper bound on the similarity score of any non-encountered documents further down the inverted lists. Therefore, as soon as $thres \leq \mathcal{R}.s_r$, the top r matching documents have been found.

To illustrate the algorithm, consider the inverted index in Figure 5.1. Suppose that the user searches for the two (i.e., $r = 2$) closest documents to the query "sleeps in the dark". The respective $w_{Q,t}$ values and inverted lists are shown in Figure 5.5. The initial $thres$ is 0.8135, based on the term scores c_1 to c_4 from the leading entries in the four inverted lists. In the first iteration, c_3 is the largest, so we pop $\langle 5, 0.265 \rangle$ from the third list. We then retrieve d_5's term frequencies to compute its score $S(d_5|Q) = 0.416$ and place $\langle 5, 0.416 \rangle$ into $\mathcal{R}$. Following that, we retrieve the next entry $\langle 3, 0.263 \rangle$ from the third list, and update $thres$ to 0.8115. After subsequent iterations pop $\langle 6, 0.200 \rangle$, $\langle 6, 0.079 \rangle$, and $\langle 6, 0.079 \rangle$, $thres$ falls below $\mathcal{R}.s_2 = 0.416$, and the algorithm terminates.

Query								
Term t	$w_{Q,t}$		**Inverted List for** t					
sleeps	2.3979	$\mapsto$	$\langle \mathbf{6, 0.079} \rangle$	$\langle \text{END}, 0 \rangle$				
in	1.0986	$\mapsto$	$\langle \mathbf{6, 0.159} \rangle$	$\langle 2, 0.148 \rangle$	$\langle 5, 0.142 \rangle$	$\langle 1, 0.058 \rangle$	$\langle 7, 0.058 \rangle$	$\langle 8, 0.053 \rangle$
			$\cdots$					
the	0.9808	$\mapsto$	$\langle \mathbf{5, 0.265} \rangle$	$\langle \mathbf{3, 0.263} \rangle$	$\langle \mathbf{6, 0.200} \rangle$	$\langle 1, 0.159 \rangle$	$\langle 2, 0.148 \rangle$	$\langle 4, 0.125 \rangle$
			$\cdots$					
dark	2.3979	$\mapsto$	$\langle \mathbf{6, 0.079} \rangle$	$\langle \text{END}, 0 \rangle$				
Result:		$=$	$\langle \mathbf{6, 0.750} \rangle$	$\langle \mathbf{5, 0.416} \rangle$				

Iteration	$thres$	Pop Entry	$\mathcal{R}$
1	0.8135	$\langle 5, 0.265 \rangle$ for 'the'	$[\langle 5, 0.416 \rangle]$
2	0.8115	$\langle 3, 0.263 \rangle$ for 'the'	$[\langle 5, 0.416 \rangle, \langle 3, 0.263 \rangle]$
3	0.7497	$\langle 6, 0.200 \rangle$ for 'the'	$[\langle 6, 0.750 \rangle, \langle 5, 0.416 \rangle]$
4	0.7095	$\langle 6, 0.079 \rangle$ for 'sleeps'	$[\langle 6, 0.750 \rangle, \langle 5, 0.416 \rangle]$
5	0.5201	$\langle 6, 0.079 \rangle$ for 'dark'	$[\langle 6, 0.750 \rangle, \langle 5, 0.416 \rangle]$
6	0.3306	Terminate	$[\langle 6, 0.750 \rangle, \langle 5, 0.416 \rangle]$

Figure 5.5: Search for top two matches to the query "sleeps in the dark" with the TRA Algorithm.

The above query processing algorithm is an adaptation of the "Threshold with Random Access" algorithm [Fagin et al., 2003]. The algorithm there examines each list to an equal depth, i.e., the same number of entries are polled from each list. This behavior is not desirable for our search engine, where some inverted lists that correspond to common words are orders of magnitude longer than those for the rarer terms. To minimize processing and authentication costs, we modify the algorithm to favor entries that contribute higher term scores c_i, so as to examine and prove as few $\langle d, f \rangle$ entries as possible from the inverted lists.

To prove that $\mathcal{R}$ satisfies the correctness criteria in Section 5.2, the search engine returns to the user a verification object (VO) that contains the following information.

- For each result document d, the VO includes the query term frequencies in d so that the user can compute the document score $S(d|Q)$.

- For each non-result document d that occurs up to the cut-off threshold in any of the inverted lists involved in the query, the VO includes the query term frequencies in d so the user can verify that its score $S(d|Q)$ is lower than those of the result documents.

- The inverted list entries that correspond to the cut-off threshold, to satisfy the user that any non-encountered documents further down in the lists cannot have similarity scores that exceed those of the result documents.

The entries that constitute the cut-off threshold are shaded in Figure 5.5, whereas those documents for which the query term frequencies are returned are highlighted in bold. We first present a simple authentication mechanism that is based on plain Merkle hash trees (MHT). After examining the pros and cons of this simple approach, we then introduce an improved Chain-MHT technique.

5.4.1 AUTHENTICATION WITH MERKLE HASH TREES

The first authentication mechanism requires the following structures. (a) A MHT is constructed over the entries in each inverted list; this structure is called *term-MHT* of that term/list. Only the document identifiers are used here; their corresponding frequencies are omitted. (b) A *document-MHT* is built for each document d, over the terms that appear in d and their corresponding frequencies. Guided by the findings of Li et al. [2006], we store only the root and the leaves of the MHTs; the intermediate digests are regenerated when they are needed at runtime. We name this the TRA-MHT mechanism (TRA query processing with MHT authentication).

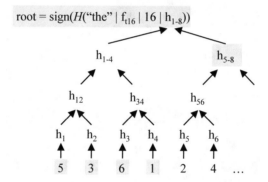

Figure 5.6: Term-MHT over the Inverted List of t_{16} ('the').

Figure 5.6 illustrates the MHT for term t_{16} ('the'). The leaves of the MHT are the document identifiers, ordered exactly as they appear in the inverted list for t_{16}. For the query in Figure 5.5, TRA has read the first four entries, which correspond to documents d_5, d_3, d_6 and d_1. To prove that these indeed are the first four entries in $\mathcal{L}_{16}$, the search engine inserts into the VO the document identifiers (i.e., numbers) 5, 3, 6, 1, the digest h_{5-8}, together with the signed root of the term-MHT. The user may verify that the entries for d_5, d_3, d_6, d_1 are the leading entries of $\mathcal{L}_{16}$ by computing $h_1 = \mathcal{H}(5), h_2 = \mathcal{H}(3), h_3 = \mathcal{H}(6), h_4 = \mathcal{H}(1)$, and combining them to derive h_{12} and h_{34}, and then h_{1-4}. Subsequently, he combines h_{1-4} with h_{5-8} (from the VO), and verifies that the derived digest matches the signed root. After verifying in this manner all the $q = 4$ inverted lists involved in $\mathcal{Q}$, the user proceeds to check the query term frequencies and compute the score of each encountered document, using its document-MHT as follows.

Consider d_6, whose document-MHT is depicted in Figure 5.7. The leaves of this MHT are the identifier-frequency pairs of all the terms in the document, in ascending identifier order.

Since the query terms are t_{15} (sleeps), t_8 (in), t_{16} (the) and t_3 (dark), the search engine adds their corresponding frequencies to the VO. The complementary digests[1] and the signed root are also included in the VO. These items are shaded in the figure. The VO items enable the user to verify the query term frequencies in d_6. Similar VO construction and verification procedures apply to all the other documents that the user needs to check (i.e., the documents whose entries are in bold in Figure 5.5). In the case where a query term does not appear in a document, the proof entails checking the pair of consecutive terms in the document-MHT that bound the query term in question. For example, if a query involves t_7 and needs to check d_6, then t_3 and t_8 are returned (together with their complementary digests). Since t_3 and t_8 are consecutive leaves in the MHT, the user is assured that d_6 does not contain t_7. The certified w_{d,Q,t_i} frequencies, combined with the f_{Q,t_i} values (which are added to the VO and verified by the root of the corresponding term-MHT, e.g., $f_{t_{16}}$ is included in the signed root of Figure 5.6), allow the user to compute/verify the score $S(d|Q)$ for each document d encountered by TRA.

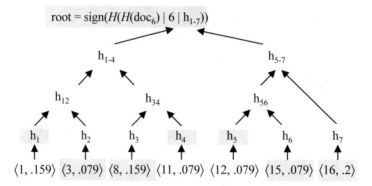

Figure 5.7: Document-MHT over d_6.

Regarding the integrity of the actual document contents, note that the root of each document-MHT includes the digest of the entire document (e.g., $\mathcal{H}(doc_6)$ in Figure 5.7). If TRA encounters a document d and $d \notin \mathcal{R}$, then the corresponding document digest is inserted into the VO. If $d \in \mathcal{R}$, its digest is not included in the VO, but is computed at the user-side during result verification. Any attempt by the server to tamper with the document content would lead to a mismatch with the signed root of the document-MHT.

The above authentication mechanism is a simple application of the Merkle Hash Tree. However, it has some serious shortcomings.

- Although TRA terminates at the cut-off threshold, the search engine has to retrieve the entire inverted lists in order to regenerate the complementary digests of the term-MHTs (e.g., h_{5-8}

---

[1]These are all the sibling digests along the path from the MHT root down to the corresponding leaf, similar to the standard MHT functionality described in Section 2.1. Note that digests common across multiple leaves need to be included only once in the VO.

in Figure 5.6). Furthermore, these digests (whose number increases with the length of the list) have to be transmitted to and processed by the user. This is particularly undesirable as some lists are extremely long (see Figure 5.3).

- The leaves of term-MHTs and document-MHTs are smaller than the upper level digests. Specifically, with 4-byte term identifiers and frequencies, a document-MHT leaf occupies 8 bytes, whereas an internal node (digest) is 16 bytes long. Instead of digests, it may be cheaper to transmit the underlying leaves; for example in Figure 5.7 it is more efficient to return all the leaves and omit the three shaded digests from the VO.

5.4.2   AUTHENTICATION WITH CHAIN MERKLE HASH TREES

The next authentication mechanism, TRA-CMHT (TRA query processing with Chain-MHTs), is designed to overcome the inefficiencies of TRA-MHT through two techniques—chain-MHT, and buddy inclusion.

To avoid retrieving and processing entire inverted lists, we observe the following.

(a) The entries in an inverted list are stored and retrieved in disk blocks. If even one entry in a block is fetched, the remaining entries in the same block are available without extra I/O cost.

(b) The inverted list is always accessed from the front. These observations lead us to the following *chain-MHT* scheme.

First, we build an embedded MHT over the inverted list entries within each block. Next, we establish a hash chain over the blocks in an inverted list. Moving from the last block towards the front, we include the digest of each block in the digest computation of the block immediately ahead of it. Finally, the digest of the first block is signed. This signature can be used to verify any j leading blocks of the inverted list, by supplying just the digest of the $j + 1$ block. The details are as follows.

Recall that l_i denotes the number of $\langle d, f \rangle$ entries in inverted list $\mathcal{L}_i$. Suppose a block holds up to ρ document identifiers (we will discuss the setting of ρ shortly), $\mathcal{L}_i$ is stored as a sequence of blocks $b_{i,1}, b_{i,2}, \ldots, b_{i,\lceil l_i/\rho \rceil}$, with $b_{i,1}$ holding the first ρ document identifiers in $\mathcal{L}_i$, $b_{i,2}$ holding the next ρ, and so on. Let $b.docid$ denote the document identifiers within block b.

$$
\begin{aligned}
digest_{i,\lceil l_i/\rho \rceil} &= MHT(b_{i,\lceil l_i/\rho \rceil}.docid) \\
digest_{i,j} &= MHT(b_{i,j}.docid + digest_{i,j+1}), \forall 1 \le j < \lceil l_i/\rho \rceil \\
\mathcal{L}_i.signature &= sign(h(\mathcal{T}.t_i \mid f_{\mathcal{T}.t_i} \mid i \mid digest_{i,1})),
\end{aligned}
$$

where $MHT(obj\text{-}list)$ returns the root digest of the Merkle hash tree over the objects in $obj\text{-}list$, and $sign(msg)$ returns a digital signature of msg. For any block $b_{i,j}$, only the root digest of its MHT is stored in the preceding block $b_{i,j-1}$. Any internal node in the MHT that is needed at runtime is regenerated dynamically from the MHT leaves in $b_{i,j}$, in order to minimize storage and retrieval overheads. The scheme is illustrated in Figure 5.8. The leaves in the MHTs here comprise only the document identifiers; their associated frequencies are stored with the document-MHTs as before.

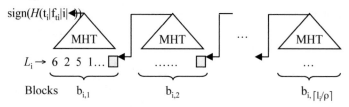

Figure 5.8: Chain of MHTs over inverted list $\mathcal{L}_i$.

With the chain-MHT, the VO for a query result contains the signature of every query term's inverted list[2]. When the query processing algorithm terminates, all the processed document identifiers in the inverted lists of the query terms are also added to the VO. In addition, for each inverted list, MHT digests that cover the unprocessed entries in the last retrieved block and the digest of the succeeding block are also computed and inserted into the VO. Consider Figure 5.6 again, but treat the MHT as being constructed over the last retrieved block of the term, rather than over the entire inverted list. The shaded digest (h_{5-8}) is the only one that is included in the VO for $\mathcal{L}_{16}$. An important advantage of the chain-MHT scheme is that the number of digests per term in the VO is only proportional to $log_2(\rho + 1)$, and is independent of the length of the inverted list. This limits the VO construction and transmission costs, as well as the user verification cost.

We now consider a realistic setting for ρ. Each block in the inverted list has to hold the disk address and digest of the succeeding block. The remaining space in the block is then reserved for the ρ document identifiers. For instance, with 1-Kbyte blocks, 4-byte document identifiers, 4-byte disk addresses and 16-byte digests, $\rho = \lfloor \frac{1024-4-16}{4} \rfloor = 251$.

Next, we turn to the second inefficiency identified in Section 5.4.1. This can be addressed through *buddy inclusion*, which works as follows. The leaves in each (document- or term-) MHT are partitioned into groups of 2^g, where g is the largest integer that satisfies $(2^g - 1) \times |\text{leaf}| \leq g \times |\text{digest}|$, $|\text{digest}|$ is the size of a digest, and $|\text{leaf}|$ is the size of a leaf. Whenever a leaf node needs to be added to the VO, its buddies in the same group are also included. To illustrate, consider Figure 5.7 where $|\text{digest}| = 16$ bytes and $|\text{leaf}| = 8$ bytes. The above inequality yields $g = 2$, so we organize the leaves into groups of $2^g = 4$. For required entry $\langle 3, 0.079 \rangle$, for instance, we additionally include in the VO its buddies $\langle 1, 0.159 \rangle$, $\langle 8, 0.159 \rangle$ and $\langle 11, 0.079 \rangle$ (this happens to cover another required entry, $\langle 8, 0.159 \rangle$). Similarly, required entry $\langle 15, 0.079 \rangle$ brings the remaining leaves into the VO. Thus, we avoid including h_1, h_4, h_5.

5.5   THRESHOLD WITH NO RANDOM ACCESS

This section introduces another query processing algorithm, called Threshold with No Random Access (TNRA). Like TRA, TNRA terminates once it determines that the top r result documents

---

[2]The list signatures could be consolidated through an aggregated signature scheme (see Section 2.1), so that only one signature is returned for the entire query result.

To find the top r matching documents for a query $\mathcal{Q}$, using a frequency-ordered inverted index.

---

(1) Initialize the sorted list $\mathcal{R}$.

(2) Fetch the first $\langle d, f \rangle$ entry in each query term t_i's inverted list $\mathcal{L}_i$.

(3) Compute $thres = \sum_{i=1}^{q} w_{\mathcal{Q}, \mathcal{Q}.t_i} \times \mathcal{L}_i.f$.

(4) While inverted list entries remain,

    (a) If the following termination conditions hold, go to step (5):

        • $\forall 1 \leq j < k \leq r, S_{LB}(\mathcal{R}.d_j | \mathcal{Q}) \geq S^{UB}(\mathcal{R}.d_k | \mathcal{Q})$;

        • $\forall j > r, S^{UB}(\mathcal{R}.d_j | \mathcal{Q}) \leq S_{LB}(\mathcal{R}.d_r | \mathcal{Q})$;

        • $S_{LB}(\mathcal{R}.d_r | \mathcal{Q}) \geq thres$.

    (b) Pop the inverted list entry $\langle d, f \rangle$ with the highest term score $c_i = w_{\mathcal{Q}, \mathcal{Q}.t_i} \times \mathcal{L}_i.f$, breaking ties arbitrarily.

    (c) If d has not been encountered before, insert $\langle d, S_{LB}(d | \mathcal{Q}), S^{UB}(d | \mathcal{Q}) \rangle$ into $\mathcal{R}$;

        else update $S_{LB}(d | \mathcal{Q})$ and $S^{UB}(d | \mathcal{Q})$ in $\mathcal{R}$.

    (d) Update $thres$ and $S^{UB}(\mathcal{R}.d_j | \mathcal{Q}) \forall \mathcal{R}.d_j$.

(5) Return the first r entries in $\mathcal{R}$ as the query result.

Figure 5.9: Threshold with No Random Access (TNRA) Algorithm.

have emerged. Unlike TRA, TNRA does not retrieve the term frequencies in the polled documents directly. Rather, it waits until enough of the term frequencies are gleamed from the inverted lists to determine the *relative* similarity scores of the polled documents.

Before introducing the algorithm, we first define some notation:

- $S^{UB}(d | \mathcal{Q})$: The upper bound of document d's similarity score with respect to query $\mathcal{Q}$ is $S^{UB}(d | \mathcal{Q}) = \sum_{i=1}^{q} w_{\mathcal{Q}, \mathcal{Q}.t_i} \times \gamma_{d, \mathcal{Q}.t_i}$ where $\gamma_{d, \mathcal{Q}.t_i} = w_{d, \mathcal{Q}.t_i}$ if d has been polled from $\mathcal{Q}.t_i$'s inverted list; otherwise $\gamma_{d, \mathcal{Q}.t_i}$ equals to the latest frequency read from that inverted list;

- $S_{LB}(d | \mathcal{Q})$: The lower bound of document d's similarity score with respect to query $\mathcal{Q}$ is $S_{LB}(d | \mathcal{Q}) = \sum_{i=1}^{q} w_{\mathcal{Q}, \mathcal{Q}.t_i} \times \gamma_{d, \mathcal{Q}.t_i}$ where $\gamma_{d, \mathcal{Q}.t_i} = w_{d, \mathcal{Q}.t_i}$ if d has been polled from $\mathcal{Q}.t_i$'s inverted list; otherwise $\gamma_{d, \mathcal{Q}.t_i} = 0$.

The TNRA algorithm ensures the correctness of query results, by checking for the following termination conditions:

- there is complete ordering among the documents in the result $\mathcal{R}$, i.e., $\forall j, k$ such that $1 \leq j < k \leq r, S_{LB}(\mathcal{R}.d_j | \mathcal{Q}) \geq S^{UB}(\mathcal{R}.d_k | \mathcal{Q})$;

- the upper bound on the score of every document d polled so far, such that $d \notin \mathcal{R}$, does not exceed the lower bound score of the last result document, i.e., $S^{UB}(d | \mathcal{Q}) \leq S_{LB}(\mathcal{R}.d_r | \mathcal{Q})$;

Query			**Inverted List for** t					
Term t	$w_{Q,t}$							
sleeps	2.3979	$\mapsto$	$\langle 6, 0.079\rangle$	$\langle \text{END}, 0\rangle$				
in	1.0986	$\mapsto$	$\langle 6, 0.159\rangle$	$\langle 2, 0.148\rangle$	$\langle 5, 0.142\rangle$	$\langle 1, 0.058\rangle$	$\langle 7, 0.058\rangle$	$\langle 8, 0.053\rangle$
			. . .					
the	0.9808	$\mapsto$	$\langle 5, 0.265\rangle$	$\langle 3, 0.263\rangle$	$\langle 6, 0.200\rangle$	$\langle 1, 0.159\rangle$	$\langle 2, 0.148\rangle$	$\langle 4, 0.125\rangle$
			. . .					
dark	2.3979	$\mapsto$	$\langle 6, 0.079\rangle$	$\langle \text{END}, 0\rangle$				
Result:		$=$	$\langle 6, 0.750\rangle$	$\langle 5, 0.416\rangle$				

Iteration	*thres*	Pop Entry	$\mathcal{R}$
1	0.814	$\langle 5, 0.265\rangle$ for 'the'	$[\langle 5, 0.260, 0.813\rangle]$
2	0.812	$\langle 3, 0.263\rangle$ for 'the'	$[\langle 5, 0.260, 0.813\rangle, \langle 3, 0.258, 0.811\rangle]$
3	0.750	$\langle 6, 0.200\rangle$ for 'the'	$[\langle 5, 0.260, 0.813\rangle, \langle 3, 0.258, 0.811\rangle, \langle 6, 0.196, 0.750\rangle]$
4	0.710	$\langle 6, 0.079\rangle$ for 'sleeps'	$[\langle 6, 0.386, 0.750\rangle, \langle 5, 0.260, 0.624\rangle, \langle 3, 0.258, 0.622\rangle]$
5	0.520	$\langle 6, 0.079\rangle$ for 'dark'	$[\langle 6, 0.575, 0.750\rangle, \langle 5, 0.260, 0.435\rangle, \langle 3, 0.258, 0.433\rangle]$
6	0.331	$\langle 6, 0.159\rangle$ for 'in'	$[\langle 6, 0.750, 0.750\rangle, \langle 5, 0.260, 0.423\rangle, \langle 3, 0.258, 0.421\rangle]$
7	0.319	$\langle 2, 0.148\rangle$ for 'in'	$[\langle 6, 0.750, 0.750\rangle, \langle 5, 0.260, 0.416\rangle, \langle 3, 0.258, 0.414\rangle,$ $\langle 2, 0.163, 0.319\rangle]$
8	0.312	$\langle 5, 0.142\rangle$ for 'in'	$[\langle 6, 0.750, 0.750\rangle, \langle 5, 0.416, 0.416\rangle, \langle 3, 0.258, 0.322\rangle,$ $\langle 2, 0.163, 0.319\rangle]$
9	0.220	Terminate	$[\langle 6, 0.750, 0.750\rangle, \langle 5, 0.416, 0.416\rangle]$

Figure 5.10: Search for top two matches to the query "sleeps in the dark" with the TNRA Algorithm.

- the threshold does not exceed the lower bound score of the last result document, i.e., *thres* $= \sum_{i=1}^{q} c_i \le S_{LB}(\mathcal{R}.d_r | Q)$.

Figure 5.9 sketches the TNRA algorithm. To illustrate, consider again the inverted index in Figure 5.1 and the query for the two closest documents to the query "sleeps in the dark". Figure 5.10 traces the execution of the algorithm. In the first iteration, c_3 is the largest, so $\langle 5, 0.265\rangle$ is popped from the third list. At this time, the lower bound for d_5's similarity score is $c_3 = 0.260$, while its upper bound is $c_1 + c_2 + c_3 + c_4 = 0.813$. The next two iterations bring d_3 and d_6 into $\mathcal{R}$. Iteration 4 pops $\langle 6, 0.079\rangle$ from the first list, so d_6's lower bound increases to $c_1 + 0.260 = 0.386$. Since the list contains no further entries, its contribution c_1 is deducted from the upper bound of all the documents in $\mathcal{R}$. The three termination conditions are satisfied only in iteration 9, whereas TRA would finish in 6 iterations as we saw previously. In general, TNRA is expected to poll a higher fraction of the inverted lists than TRA. The advantage of TNRA is that it avoids the I/O cost of fetching immediately the term frequencies in the polled documents.

The TNRA algorithm here is an adaptation of the "Threshold with No Random Access" algorithm [Fagin et al., 2003]. Again, the algorithm there examines each list to an equal depth, i.e., the same number of entries are polled from each list. In contrast, our adaptation favors those inverted lists that contribute higher term scores c_i, and is more appropriate for text search engines in which some inverted lists are orders of magnitude longer than others.

To support query result authentication for TNRA, the search engine has to include in the VO the $\langle d, f \rangle$ entries, from the front down to the cut-off threshold in each inverted list. The cut-off threshold in each list, shaded in Figure 5.10, must add up to the overall threshold. If the search engine were to return a wrong query answer, it would have to be substantiated by altering either the value in some $\langle d, f \rangle$ entries or the order of the entries within some inverted list. However, any such alteration would cause a mismatch with the signature of the corresponding inverted list(s), so the user would be able to detect that the answer is wrong.

Like TRA, TNRA can be coupled with MHT or CMHT. However, we do not require separate document-MHTs here. Instead, we incorporate the term frequencies into the term-MHT or chain-MHT, so each leaf node is a pair of a document identifier and its term frequency. Figure 5.11 illustrates the modified CMHT structure. The VO construction and verification procedures remain the same as those of TRA. The number of entries per block, ρ', is computed similarly to ρ in Section 5.4.2, the difference being that now each leaf is (and has the size of) an identifier-frequency pair.

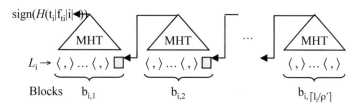

Figure 5.11: Chain-MHT for the TNRA Algorithm.

Finally, we discuss a space optimization technique that is applicable to both TRA and TNRA. In the methods as presented so far, the search engine stores one signature for every inverted list. We can reduce this number down to one, at the expense of a larger VO size. Specifically, we can build an implicit (i.e., computed-on-demand) dictionary-MHT on top of the root digests of the individual term-MHTs or chain-MHTs, and sign only the root of the dictionary-MHT. Although this approach reduces the space requirements, it leads to additional digests in the VO (from the dictionary-MHT). This trade-off is not very appealing in general, since the signature size is negligible compared to that of the documents themselves. It may, however, be useful in extreme cases where the search engine has insufficient storage.

5.6   SUMMARY

In this chapter, we presented a mechanism for verifying the query results generated by text search engines. The aim is to enable the users to detect whether their search results indeed contain the most relevant documents, ranked in the right order, and include no spurious entries; in short, whether their search results are the same as what an intact system would produce. We formulate the properties that define a correct search result, map the task of processing a text search query to adaptations of existing threshold-based algorithms, and devise authentication mechanisms for verifying correctness of the results.

Document retrieval often employs complementary mechanisms to improve effectiveness. For instance, Web search engines may exploit the document metadata or the hyperlink structure among documents to boost the ranking of the authoritative documents (e.g. [Brin and Page, 1998, Kleinberg, 1999]). Extending the authentication framework to capture such elaborate ranking mechanisms is a promising direction for future work.

CHAPTER 6

Data Streams

Electronic services like stock trading, online bidding, RFID-enabled supply chain management, environment sensing and monitoring, have become commonplace, especially with the widespread adoption of mobile devices like smart-phones and tablet PCs. Such services can generate large streams of data, and they are often delivered over intermediary platforms (e.g., brokerages) to the end-users. It is thus necessary to verify that the delivered data streams are authentic and complete.

- *Authentic*: A data stream is authentic if every datum in it originated from the source, and no spurious data are introduced en-route. Moreover, the data retain their original relative order in the stream.

- *Complete*: Every datum in the stream is delivered.

In this chapter, we describe techniques proposed by Li et al. [2007] and Papadopoulos et al. [2007] for authenticating data streams.

6.1   DATA STREAM MODEL

A data stream S is an infinite sequence of tuples, $S = (d_1, d_2, \ldots)$, in which tuple d_{i+1} arrives immediately after tuple d_i. The tuples share a common schema $\langle A_1, A_2, \ldots, A_m \rangle$.

A window query over a data stream may be one-shot, or of the sliding window variety. A *one-shot window query* reports an answer computed once over a user-defined temporal range. Such a query takes the form:

SELECT * FROM Stream
WHERE $l_i \leq A_i \leq u_i$
WINDOW SIZE n

whereas a one-shot aggregation window query over attribute A_i, $1 \leq i \leq m$, is:

SELECT AGGR(A_i) FROM Stream
WHERE $l_i \leq A_i \leq u_1$
WINDOW SIZE n

where AGGR is a distributive aggregate function like SUM, COUNT, MIN, MAX. In the worst case, the user will receive query answers b tuple arrivals after issuing the query.

The second type of data stream query incorporates the notion of sliding window. The sliding window reflects the interest of the user in the newest available tuples, and may be defined in two alternative ways. A *count*-based window contains the n most recent tuples for some constant number

N, whereas a *time*-based window contains only tuples that arrived within the last n time units. The maximum tolerable delay to receive the (latest) query answer is b time units.

A *sliding window query* reports answers continuously as they change, over user-defined window sizes and update intervals. The form of a selection sliding window query is:

SELECT * FROM Stream
WHERE $l_i \leq A_i \leq u_i$
WINDOW SIZE n, SLIDE EVERY σ

whereas an aggregation sliding window query over attribute A_i, $1 \leq i \leq m$, is:

SELECT AGGR(A_i) FROM Stream
WHERE $l_i \leq A_i \leq u_i$
WINDOW SIZE n, SLIDE EVERY σ

The server constructs the initial answer for a sliding window query by treating it like a one-shot query. Thereafter, the server incrementally communicates any changes to the user, as tuples expire from the window and new tuples enter the window. The user will receive updates with at most a b-tuple delay.

6.2   TUMBLING MERKLE TREE

In this chapter, we focus on the Tumbling Merkle Tree (TM-tree) [Li et al., 2007] for authenticating selection-aggregation queries over a single attribute of interest, A. There are extensions of the technique for multi-dimensional queries and one-shot queries, but we do not discuss those in this book.

6.2.1   TM-TREE CONSTRUCTION

Suppose that the system-wide maximum window size is N (meaning that all user queries must have window size $n < N$) and the maximum tolerable response delay is b, only the $N + b$ most recent tuples in $\mathcal{S}$ are of interest. The data owner builds a Merkle hash tree (MHT) for every successive b tuples; this produces $\lceil N/b \rceil + 1$ MHTs. Within each MHT, the tuples are ordered by their A values. The signature of each MHT incorporates its root digest, as well as the timestamp of the oldest and newest tuples within the tree, i.e., the signature is $s(\mathcal{H}(h_{root}|t_L|t_U))$ where s is a signing operation using the owner's private key, h_{root} is the root digest of the MHT, t_L and t_H are the timestamp of the oldest and newest tuples in the MHT, respectively. The resulting structure, called Tumbling Merkle Tree (TM-tree), is distributed to the query server.

Figure 6.1 gives an illustration of the TM-tree. In the figure, tuples are represented as dots, positioned according to their arrival time (on the x-axis) and attribute value (on the y-axis). N_b of the tuples are organized into $\lceil N/b \rceil + 1$ MHTs, denoted as rectangles in dashed lines. On the right end, two of the newest tuples have yet to be incorporated into any MHT. The rectangle in green outline represents a query, with its height and width corresponding to the selection range and window size, respectively.

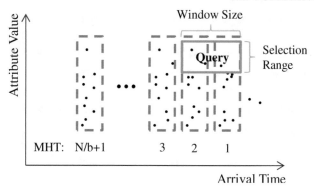

Figure 6.1: Tumbling Merkle Tree.

After the initial construction, the TM-tree is updated after every b tuple arrivals. Specifically, the data owner and the server separately build a MHT for the b new tuples. Additionally, the owner signs the MHT and forwards the signature to the server, after which the two parties discard the oldest MHT.

6.2.2   ONE-SHOT SELECTION QUERIES

On receiving a one-shot selection query with window size n, the server delays until the latest tuple is included in a completed MHT; this delay is at most $b - 1$ tuple arrivals. Then, for each of the $\lceil n/b \rceil + 1$ most recent MHTs, the server returns the tuples that meet the selection condition plus the boundary tuples (to prove completeness, as explained in Section 3.2.2), along with the complementary verification object (VO). The timestamps t_L, t_H, and the signature of each MHT are also returned to the user.

In verifying the query answer, the user checks the following conditions.

- In each MHT, the returned tuples cover the selection range and they combine with the VO to match the signature.

- The timestamps of the MHTs indicate that they cover the n most recent tuples.

- Among the returned MHTs, the latest is indeed the most current one in the data stream.

The oldest returned MHT may include false positive—tuples that are beyond the window size. After the MHT is verified, the user will have to filter out the false positives. By construction, the number of false positives is at most $b - 1$.

6.2.3   SLIDING WINDOW SELECTION QUERIES

In the case of a sliding window selection query that slides every σ tuple arrivals, the server produces an initial answer by processing it as a one-shot query. This entails a delay of up to $b - 1$ tuple arrivals.

Thereafter, the server needs to update the answer after every σ tuple arrivals. Note that σ cannot be less than b.

Every time the server has a completed MHT over the new tuples, it checks whether the query's sliding period has expired. If so, the server constructs a VO for the user that contains the tuples that have expired from the query window, and the new tuples that have arrived since the last update. The expired tuples are localized within the (at most) $\lceil \sigma/b \rceil + 1$ Merkle trees at the left boundary of the sliding window. Similarly, the new tuples are localized in the (at most) $\lceil \sigma/b \rceil + 1$ Merkle trees that are created since the last update. The update mechanism does not require the server to maintain detailed state information for the query, thus promoting scalability.

6.2.4   AGGREGATION QUERIES

The TM-tree can be adapted easily to support aggregation queries. Specifically, each internal node of an MHT is associated with the aggregate value over the tuples in the underlying subtree, and the node digest takes into account this aggregate value besides the child digests. In answering a query, the covering leaf and internal nodes that span the selection range in each MHT are returned to the user, along with the complementary VO. After verifying the returned nodes, the user then combine the node values into the desired aggregate. The adaptation is similar to the aggregate authentication mechanism that we introduced in Section 3.5.

6.3   CONTINUOUS MONITORING OF TUPLES IN A SELECTION RANGE

Instead of the notion of sliding window, some applications may only need to allow users to verify the arrival, removal and update of tuples that fall within a certain selection range on a common attribute A. In this section, we describe another data stream authentication mechanism based on the CADS method [Papadopoulos et al., 2007]. We use the example in Figure 6.2 to aid in the explanation

Suppose that the domain of A is $[\mathcal{L}, \mathcal{U}]$. The data owner begins by calving the domain into partitions. In Figure 6.2, the domain $[0, 80]$ is partitioned into $[0, 20]$, $(20, 40]$, $(40, 60]$, $(60, 80]$. The tuples that fall within each partition are organized in a Temporal Merkle Hash Tree (TMH-tree), thus we have TMH_1, TMH_2, TMH_3 and TMH_4 for the four partitions. The TMH-tree modifies the MHT to include a timestamp in each node that tracks the time of the latest tuple change in the underlying subtree. Together with the child digests, the timestamp of each node determine its digest.

On top of the partitions, the owner constructs another MHT, called the Domain Partition Merkle-tree (DPM-tree). Each leaf node of the DPM-tree corresponds to one partition, and contains two timestamps LT and PT tracking the latest and penultimate tuple changes in that partition. The digest of a leaf node is derived from the root digest of that partition's TMH-tree and the two timestamps. Each internal node of the DPM-tree is augmented with a timestamp LT on the latest tuple change in the subtree underneath. The digest of an internal DPM-tree node is derived

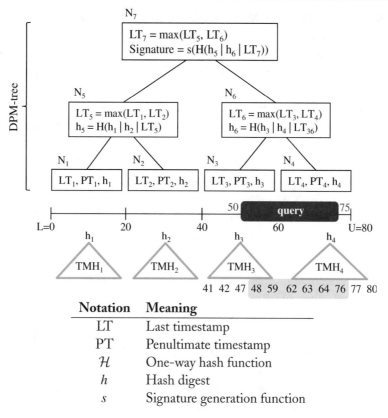

Notation	Meaning
LT	Last timestamp
PT	Penultimate timestamp
$\mathcal{H}$	One-way hash function
h	Hash digest
s	Signature generation function

Figure 6.2: Example of DPM-Tree and TMH-Tree.

from hashing the concatenation of its child digests and timestamp. With the owner's private key, a signature is computed on the root digest of the DPM-tree. The DPM-tree, its signature and the TMH-trees are then distributed to the query server. Thereafter, the owner continues to update the DPM-tree, its signature and the TMH-trees whenever there are tuple changes.

For each monitoring query, the server generates an initial answer with a VO for the user. In our running example in Figure 6.2, we have a range selection $50 \leq A \leq 75$. This is done by processing the DPM-tree from the root down to the leaf level. For each node encountered, the server checks whether its range coverage overlaps the selection range of the query. If so, the node's timestamp LT (and PT if applicable) is added to the VO, then the server traverses down the node (e.g., N_7 followed by N_6); otherwise the node's digest is added to the VO (e.g., digest h_5 for N_5). Upon reaching the leaf level of the DPM-tree, the server proceeds down the TMH-tree (TMH$_3$ and TMH$_4$) for the partition corresponding to each traversed leaf node (N_3 and N_4, respectively). From each TMH-tree, the qualifying tuples are added to the query answer while their complementary digests are added to the VO; this step is similar to the MHT-based selection authentication mechanism described in Section 3.2.2. The qualifying tuples are marked by a gray rectangle in the figure. Finally, the signature of the DPM-tree is added to the VO. The query answer is complete provided the result tuples span consecutive partitions and hence leaf nodes of the DPM-tree, and the boundary tuples (with key values 48 and 76, respectively, in the example) envelop the selection range of the query.

After the initial answer, the server will update the user on tuple changes that fall into the selection range of the query, along with the complementary digests for verifying the changes. Proceeding down the DPM-tree, the user will expect an update under every internal node that overlaps the query range unless its timestamp is older than t, the time of the last update received by the user. For each DPM-tree leaf node overlapping the query range that is updated after t, the user will check the penultimate timestamp of that leaf node; this timestamp should be no later than t, otherwise the server has omitted at least one prior tuple update in the corresponding partition.

6.4   SUMMARY

This chapter described techniques for authenticating data streams. In the case of queries that monitor the arrival, removal and update of tuples with attribute value falling within some user-specified range, we have a method based on CADS [Papadopoulos et al., 2007] that avoids sending updates that do not affect the query answer. We also have a Tumbling Merkle Tree scheme [Li et al., 2007] that supports user-specified sliding windows, in addition to query ranges.

Both of the schemes are built on the Merkle hash tree. It would be interesting to develop their counterparts based on signature aggregation. Furthermore, the Tumbling Merkle Tree scheme allows new tuples to be released to users only in batches, thus imposing a response delay. Adaptations or alternative designs that minimize this response delay would be meaningful endeavors.

CHAPTER 7

Conclusion

In data publishing, owners outsource their data and processing logics to a third-party publisher. This raises security concerns. In particular, there is a need to ensure users that answers to their queries are correct. In this book, we focused on solutions for authenticating query answers. The basic idea is for the publisher to also return the query answer together with an additional set of verification objects. With the verification objects, the users can verify that the answers are authentic, complete and correct.

We reviewed existing works on query authentication in various domains, including relational databases, spatial databases, text search, and data streams, These solutions can be broadly categorized into Merkle Hash Tree-based and signature-based.

For each domain, we highlighted directions for promising research in the respective chapters. In addition, there are several other emerging trends that are worth pursuing.

1. **Query execution assurance.** Very often, it is necessary to perform compute-intensive operations on a large amount of data, e.g., data mining. In these cases, it is not practical to generate verification objects for authenticating the answers. Instead, an alternative approach that shows proofs that the operations have been performed would be more effective. One such mechanism, based on a challenge-response approach, is developed by Sion [2005]. The mechanism batches a set of queries for processing at the third party publisher. In addition, it computes one or more challenge tokens that are also submitted to the publisher. These challenge tokens are based on users' actual execution of the same operations. The publisher will evaluate the queries, and produce the execution proofs based on the challenge tokens. Note that the execution proofs can only be correct if the actual executions are performed, Upon receiving the answers to all queries, and the execution proofs, the user is able to verify, with high probability, if the queries have been actually processed (by comparing the challenge tokens with the execution proofs). More work can be done to develop effective and efficient methods with stronger non-probabilistic guarantees.

2. **Querying encrypted data.** So far, we assumed that the data stored at the third party publisher are in the plain. For some critical and/or sensitive data, it may be necessary to encrypt the data so that the publisher cannot "see" the actual content. This calls for novel query processing methods that can operate on encrypted data. Existing works [Boneh and Waters, 2007, Hacigümüs et al., 2002, Shi et al., 2007] offer some preliminary results that are promising. However, these methods do not deal with query authentication. It will be interesting to explore how queries on encrypted data can be authenticated.

3. **Data publishing model.** In this book, we considered a data publishing model where the data owner and the publisher are required to maintain authenticated data structures to enable query authentication. Recently, Papadopoulos et al. [2009] propose a novel model called SAE that separates authentication from query execution. Under SAE, the data owner only needs to maintain the dataset as a result of updates, while the publisher only stores the data (without the authenticated data structures) and performs query processing as in conventional server. However, a trusted entity is introduced to handle all security-related tasks. The user interacts with the trusted entity to establish the correctness of the results returned by the publisher. More investigation is needed to study the relationship between the owner, the publisher and the trusted entity in order to fine tune the design of a acceptable data publishing model.

Bibliography

Pankaj K. Agarwal, Mark de Berg, Joachim Gudmundsson, Mikael Hammar, and Herman J. Haverkort. Box-trees and R-trees with near-optimal query time. *Discrete & Computational Geometry*, 28(3):291–312, 2002. DOI: 10.1007/s00454-002-2817-1 Cited on page(s) 42

Ross Anderson, Roger Needham, and Adi Shamir. The steganographic file system. In *Information Hiding*, volume 1525 of *Lecture Notes in Computer Science*, pages 73–82. Springer Berlin / Heidelberg, 1998. DOI: 10.1007/3-540-49380-8_6 Cited on page(s) 3

Michael Aschbacher. *Finite Group Theory, Second Edition*. Cambridge University Press, 2000. Cited on page(s) 6

Norbert Beckmann, Hans-Peter Kriegel, Ralf Schneider, and Bernhard Seeger. The R*-Tree: an efficient and robust access method for points and rectangles. In Hector Garcia-Molina and H. V. Jagadish, editors, *Proc. ACM SIGMOD Int. Conf. on Management of Data*, pages 322–331. ACM Press, 1990. Cited on page(s) 40, 52

Josh Benaloh and Michael de Mare. One-way accumulators: A decentralized alternative to digital signatures. In *Proc. Int. Conf. Theory and Application of Cryptographic Techniques*, pages 274–285, 1993. DOI: 10.1007/3-540-48285-7_24 Cited on page(s) 5

Jon L. Bentley. Multidimensional binary search trees used for associative searching. *Commun. ACM*, 18(9):509–517, 1975. DOI: 10.1145/361002.361007 Cited on page(s) 37

Elisa Bertino, Barbara Carminati, Elena Ferrari, Bhavani M. Thuraisingham, and Amar Gupta. Selective and authentic third-party distribution of XML documents. *IEEE Trans. Knowl. and Data Eng.*, 16(10):1263–1278, 2004. DOI: 10.1109/TKDE.2004.63 Cited on page(s) 12

Burton Bloom. Space/time trade-offs in hash coding with allowable errors. *Commun. ACM*, 13(7): 422–426, July 1970. DOI: 10.1145/362686.362692 Cited on page(s) 8, 23

Dan Boneh and Brent Waters. Conjunctive, subset, and range queries on encrypted data. In *Proc 4th Conference on Theory of Cryptography*, pages 535–554, 2007. DOI: 10.1007/978-3-540-70936-7_29 Cited on page(s) 79

Dan Boneh, Ben Lynn, and Hovav Shacham. Short signatures from the weil pairing. In *Proc. 7th Int. Conf. Theory and Application of Cryptology and Information Security*, pages 514–532, 2001. DOI: 10.1007/s00145-004-0314-9 Cited on page(s) 7

Dan Boneh, Craig Gentry, Ben Lynn, and Hovav Shacham. A survey of two signature aggregation techniques. *CryptoBytes*, 6(2):1–10, 2003. Cited on page(s) 5, 7

Sergey Brin and Lawrence Page. The anatomy of a large-scale hypertextual web search engine. *Computer Networks and ISDN Systems*, 30(1–7):107–117, 1998. DOI: 10.1016/S0169-7552(98)00110-X Cited on page(s) 72

Certicom. SEC2: Recommended elliptic curve domain parameters, version 1.0. *Standards for Efficient Cryptography*, September 2000. `http://www.secg.org/download/aid-386/sec2_final.pdf`. Cited on page(s) 6

Weiwei Cheng and Kian-Lee Tan. Authenticating kNN query results in data publishing. In *Secure Data Management*, pages 47–63, 2007. DOI: 10.1007/978-3-540-75248-6_4 Cited on page(s) 40, 50, 52

Weiwei Cheng and Kian-Lee Tan. Query assurance verification for outsourced multi-dimensional databases. *J. Computer Security*, 17(1):101–126, 2009. Cited on page(s) 13, 40, 42, 50, 53

Weiwei Cheng, HweeHwa Pang, and Kian-Lee Tan. Authenticating multi-dimensional query results in data publishing. In *Proc. IFIP TC11/ WG11.3 20th Annual Working Conf. on Database Security*, pages 60–73, 2006. DOI: 10.1007/11805588_5 Cited on page(s) 13, 40, 42, 46

Santosh Chokani. Trusted products evaluation. *Commun. ACM*, 35(7):64–76, 1992. DOI: 10.1145/129902.129907 Cited on page(s) 3

Seok-Ju Chun, Chin-Wan Chung, Ju-Hong Lee, and Seok-Lyong Lee. Dynamic update cube for range-sum queries. In *Proc. 27th Int. Conf. on Very Large Data Bases*, pages 521–530, 2001. Cited on page(s) 34

Douglas Comer. Ubiquitous B-tree. *ACM Comput. Surv.*, 11(2):121–137, 1979. DOI: 10.1145/356770.356776 Cited on page(s) 13

Premkumar T. Devanbu, Michael Gertz, Charles U. Martel, and Stuart G. Stubblebine. Authentic third-party data publication. In *Proc. IFIP TC11/ WG11.3 14th Annual Working Conf. on Database Security*, pages 101–112, 2000. Cited on page(s) 1

Premkumar T. Devanbu, Michael Gertz, Charles U. Martel, and Stuart G. Stubblebine. Authentic data publication over the internet. *J. Computer Security*, 11(3):291–314, 2003. Cited on page(s) 12, 39

Ronald Fagin, Amnon Lotem, and Moni Naor. Optimal aggregation algorithms for middleware. *J. Comp. and System Sci.*, 66(4):614–656, 2003. DOI: 10.1016/S0022-0000(03)00026-6 Cited on page(s) 64, 70

Hakan Ferhatosmanoglu, Ioanna Stanoi, Divyakant Agrawal, and Amr El Abbadi. Constrained nearest neighbor queries. In *Proc. 7th Int. Symp. Advances in Spatial and Temporal Databases*, pages 257–278, 2001. Cited on page(s) 52

Steven Geffner, Divakant Agrawal, and Amr El Abbadi. The dynamic data cube. In *Advances in Database Technology, Proc. 7th Int. Conf. on Extending Database Technology*, pages 237–253, 2000. Cited on page(s) 34

Michael T. Goodrich, Roberto Tamassia, and Jasminka Hasic. An efficient dynamic and distributed cryptographic accumulator. In *Proc. 5th Int. Conf. on Information Security*, pages 372–388, 2002. DOI: 10.1007/3-540-45811-5_29 Cited on page(s) 5

Michael T. Goodrich, Roberto Tamassia, and Nikos Triandopoulos. Super-efficient verification of dynamic outsourced databases. In *Proc. The Cryptographers' Track at the RSA Conference 2008*, pages 407–424, 2008. DOI: 10.1007/978-3-540-79263-5_26 Cited on page(s) 13

Jim Gray, Surajit Chaudhuri, Adam Bosworth, Andrew Layman, Don Reichart, Murali Venkatrao, Frank Pellow, and Hamid Pirahesh. Data cube: A relational aggregation operator generalizing group-by, cross-tab, and sub-totals. *Proc. ACM SIGMOD Workshop on Research Issues in Data Mining and Knowledge Discovery*, 1:29–53, 1997. DOI: 10.1023/A:1009726021843 Cited on page(s) 32

Antonin Guttman. R-trees: A dynamic index structure for spatial searching. In *Proc. ACM SIGMOD Int. Conf. on Management of Data*, pages 47–57, 1984. DOI: 10.1145/971697.602266 Cited on page(s) 37

Hakan Hacigumus, Bala Iyer, and Sharad Mehrotra. Providing database as a service. In *Proc. 18th Int. Conf. on Data Engineering*, pages 29–38, 2002. DOI: 10.1109/ICDE.2002.994695 Cited on page(s) 1

Hakan Hacigümüs, Balakrishna R. Iyer, Chen Li, and Sharad Mehrotra. Executing SQL over encrypted data in the database-service-provider model. In *Proc. ACM SIGMOD Int. Conf. on Management of Data*, pages 216–227, 2002. DOI: 10.1145/564691.564717 Cited on page(s) 79

Ching-Tien Ho, Rakesh Agrawal, Nimrod Megiddo, and Ramakrishnan Srikant. Range queries in OLAP data cubes. In *Proc. ACM SIGMOD Int. Conf. on Management of Data*, pages 73–88, 1997. DOI: 10.1145/253260.253274 Cited on page(s) 33

Ling Hu, Wei-Shinn Ku, Spiridon Bakiras, and Cyrus Shahabi. Verifying spatial queries using Voronoi neighbors. In *Proc. 18th SIGSPATIAL ACM Int. Symp. on Advances in Geographic Information Systems*, pages 350–359, 2010. DOI: 10.1145/1869790.1869839 Cited on page(s) 47

Ryan Huebsch, Joseph M. Hellerstein, Nick Lanham, Boon Thau Loo, Scott Shenker, and Ion Stoica. Querying the internet with PIER. In *Proc. 29th Int. Conf. on Very Large Data Bases*, pages 321–332, 2003. Cited on page(s) 1

Antoine Joux and Kim Nguyen. Separating decision Diffie-Hellman from computational Diffie-Hellman in cryptographic groups. *J. Cryptology*, 16(4):239–247, 2003. DOI: 10.1007/s00145-003-0052-4 Cited on page(s) 7

Jon M. Kleinberg. Authoritative sources in a hyperlinked environment. *J. ACM*, 46(5):604–632, 1999. DOI: 10.1145/324133.324140 Cited on page(s) 72

Arjen K. Lenstra and Eric R. Verheul. Selecting cryptographic key sizes. *J. Cryptology*, 14:255–293, 2001. DOI: 10.1007/s00145-001-0009-4 Cited on page(s) 8

Feifei Li, Marios Hadjieleftheriou, George Kollios, and Leonid Reyzin. Dynamic authenticated index structures for outsourced databases. In *Proc. ACM SIGMOD Int. Conf. on Management of Data*, pages 121–132, 2006. DOI: 10.1145/1142473.1142488 Cited on page(s) 3, 13, 16, 65

Feifei Li, Ke Yi, Marios Hadjieleftheriou, and George Kollios. Proof-infused streams: Enabling authentication of sliding window queries on streams. In *Proc. 33rd Int. Conf. on Very Large Data Bases*, pages 147–158, 2007. Cited on page(s) 73, 74, 78

Qiong Luo, Sailesh Krishnamurthy, C. Mohan, Hamid Pirahesh, Honguk Woo, Bruce G. Lindsay, and Jeffrey F. Naughton. Middle-tier database caching for e-business. In *Proc. ACM SIGMOD Int. Conf. on Management of Data*, pages 600–611, 2002. DOI: 10.1145/564691.564763 Cited on page(s) 1

David L. Margulius. Apps on the edge. *InfoWorld*, 24(21), May 2002. Cited on page(s) 1

Charles U. Martel, Glen Nuckolls, Premkumar T. Devanbu, Michael Gertz, April Kwong, and Stuart G. Stubblebine. A general model for authenticated data structures. *Algorithmica*, 39(1): 21–41, 2004. DOI: 10.1007/s00453-003-1076-8 Cited on page(s) 6

Ralph C. Merkle. A certified digital signature. In *Crypto*, pages 218–238, 1989. Cited on page(s) 6

Gerome Miklau and Dan Suciu. Controlling access to published data using cryptography. In *Proc. 29th Int. Conf. on Very Large Data Bases*, pages 898–909, 2003. Cited on page(s) 1

Kyriakos Mouratidis, Dimitris Sacharidis, and HweeHwa Pang. Partially materialized digest scheme: An efficient verification method for outsourced databases. *Proc. 35th Int. Conf. on Very Large Data Bases*, 18(1):363–381, 2009. DOI: 10.1007/s00778-008-0108-z Cited on page(s) 13, 17

Einar Mykletun, Maithili Narasimha, and Gene Tsudik. Signature bouquets: Immutability for aggregated/condensed signatures. In *Proc. 9th European Symp. on Research in Computer Security*, pages 160–176, 2004. Cited on page(s) 47

Einar Mykletun, Maithili Narasimha, and Gene Tsudik. Authentication and integrity in outsourced databases. *ACM Trans. Storage*, 2(2):107–138, May 2006. DOI: 10.1145/1149976.1149977 Cited on page(s) 8, 47

Maithili Narasimha and Gene Tsudik. Authentication of outsourced databases using signature aggregation and chaining. In *Proc. 11th Int. Conf. on Database Systems for Advanced Applications*, pages 420–436, 2006. DOI: 10.1007/11733836_30 Cited on page(s) 13, 23

National Security Agency. The case for elliptic curve cryptography, 2009a. URL http://www.nsa.gov/business/programs/elliptic_curve.shtml. [Online; accessed January 2012]. Cited on page(s) 8

National Security Agency. NSA suite B cryptography, 2009b. URL http://www.nsa.gov/ia/programs/suiteb_cryptography/. [Online; accessed January 2012]. Cited on page(s) 8

B. Clifford Neuman and Theodore Ts'o. Kerberos: An authentication service for computer networks. *IEEE Commun. Mag.*, 32(9):33–38, 1994. DOI: 10.1109/35.312841 Cited on page(s) 3

Jurg Nievergelt, Hans Hinterberger, and Kenneth C. Sevcik. The grid file: An adaptable, symmetric multikey file structure. *ACM Trans. Database Syst.*, 9(1):38–71, March 1984. DOI: 10.1145/348.318586 Cited on page(s) 45

Glen Nuckolls. Verified query results from hybrid authentication trees. In *Proc. IFIP TC11/ WG11.3 19th Annual Working Conf. on Database Security*, pages 84–98, 2005. Cited on page(s) 13

HweeHwa Pang and Kyriakos Mouratidis. Authenticating the query results of text search engines. In *Proc. 34th Int. Conf. on Very Large Data Bases*, pages 126–137, 2008. DOI: 10.1145/1453856.1453875 Cited on page(s) 57, 62

HweeHwa Pang and Kian-Lee Tan. Authenticating query results in edge computing. In *Proc. 20th Int. Conf. on Data Engineering*, pages 560–571, 2004. DOI: 10.1109/ICDE.2004.1320027 Cited on page(s) 12

HweeHwa Pang and Kian-Lee Tan. Verifying completeness of relational query answers from online servers. *ACM Trans. Information System Security*, 11(2):1–50, 2008. DOI: 10.1145/1330332.1330337 Cited on page(s) 18, 26, 27, 29, 61

HweeHwa Pang, Kian-Lee Tan, and Xuan Zhou. StegFS: A steganographic file system. In *Proc. 19th Int. Conf. on Data Engineering*, pages 657–668, March 2003. DOI: 10.1109/ICDE.2003.1260829 Cited on page(s) 3

HweeHwa Pang, Arpit Jain, Krithi Ramamritham, and Kian-Lee Tan. Verifying completeness of relational query results in data publishing. In *Proc. ACM SIGMOD Int. Conf. on Management of Data*, pages 407–418, 2005. DOI: 10.1145/1066157.1066204 Cited on page(s) 13, 18, 42

HweeHwa Pang, Jilian Zhang, and Kyriakos Mouratidis. Scalable verification for outsourced dynamic databases. In *Proc. 35th Int. Conf. on Very Large Data Bases*, pages 802–813, 2009. DOI: 10.1145/1066157.1066204 Cited on page(s) 8, 13, 23

Stavros Papadopoulos, Yin Yang, and Dimitris Papadias. CADS: Continuous authentication on data streams. In *Proc. 33rd Int. Conf. on Very Large Data Bases*, pages 135–146, 2007. Cited on page(s) 73, 76, 78

Stavros Papadopoulos, Dimitris Papadias, Weiwei Cheng, and Kian-Lee Tan. Separating authentication from query execution in outsourced databases. In *Proc. 25th Int. Conf. on Data Engineering*, pages 1148–1151, 2009. DOI: 10.1109/ICDE.2009.187 Cited on page(s) 80

Charles P. Pfleeger and Shari Lawrence Pfleeger. *Security in Computing*. Prentice Hall, 3 edition, 2003. Cited on page(s) 57

Bartosz Przydatek, Dawn Song, and Adrian Perrig. SIA: Secure information aggregation in sensor networks. In *Proc. 1st Int. Conf. on Embedded Networked Sensor Systems*, pages 255–265, 2003. DOI: 10.1145/958491.958521 Cited on page(s) 34

Ron L. Rivest, Adi Shamir, and Leonard M. Adleman. A method for obtaining digital signatures and public-key cryptosystems. *Commun. ACM*, 21(2):120–126, 1978. DOI: 10.1145/359340.359342 Cited on page(s) 5, 6, 8

Hans Sagan. *Space-Filling Curves*. Springer-Verlag, New York, 1994. DOI: 10.1007/978-1-4612-0871-6 Cited on page(s) 42

Hanan Samet. The quadtree and related hierarchical data structures. *ACM Comput. Surv.*, 16: 187–260, 1984. DOI: 10.1145/356924.356930 Cited on page(s) 45

Ravi S. Sandhu and Pierangela Samarati. Access control: Principles and practice. *IEEE Commun. Mag.*, 32(9):40–48, 1994. DOI: 10.1109/35.312842 Cited on page(s) 2, 3

Stefan Saroiu, Krishna P. Gummadi, Richard J. Dunn, Steven D. Gribble, and Henry M. Levy. An analysis of internet content delivery systems. In *Proc. 5th USENIX Symp. on Operating System Design and Implementation*, pages 315–327, 2002. DOI: 10.1145/1060289.1060319 Cited on page(s) 1

SHA. *Secure Hashing Algorithm*. NIST. FIPS 180-2, 2001. Cited on page(s) 5

Elaine Shi, John Bethencourt, Hubert T.-H. Chan, Dawn Xiaodong Song, and Adrian Perrig. Multi-dimensional range query over encrypted data. In *Proc. 2010 IEEE Symposium on Security and Privacy*, pages 350–364, 2007. DOI: 10.1109/SP.2007.29 Cited on page(s) 79

Radu Sion. Query execution assurance for outsourced databases. In *Proc. 31st Int. Conf. on Very Large Data Bases*, pages 601–612, 2005. Cited on page(s) 79

Yin Yang, Stavros Papadopoulos, Dimitris Papadias, and George Kollios. Authenticated indexing for outsourced spatial databases. *VLDB J.*, 18(3):631–648, 2009. DOI: 10.1007/s00778-008-0113-2 Cited on page(s) 37, 40, 42

Cui Yu, Beng Chin Ooi, Kian-Lee Tan, and H. V. Jagadish. Indexing the distance: An efficient method to KNN processing. In *Proc. 27th Int. Conf. on Very Large Data Bases*, pages 421–430, 2001. Cited on page(s) 37, 52

Justin Zobel and Alistair Moffat. Inverted files for text search engine. *ACM Comput. Surv.*, 38(2): 6, July 2006. DOI: 10.1145/1132956.1132959 Cited on page(s) 57, 58, 59

Authors' Biographies

HWEEHWA PANG

HweeHwa Pang is a Professor of Information Systems at the School of Information Systems, Singapore Management University. He obtained his Ph.D. in Computer Science from the University of Wisconsin-Madison in 1994. He has extensive experience in applied research and development, and in technology commercialization. His current research interests include data privacy and security, social network analysis, query processing on high-dimensional data, and information retrieval. He publishes actively in leading conferences and journals in databases and in information security.

KIAN-LEE TAN

Kian-Lee Tan is a Professor of Computer Science at the School of Computing, National University of Singapore (NUS). He received his Ph.D. in computer science in 1994 from NUS. His current research interests include multimedia information retrieval, query processing and optimization in multiprocessor and distributed systems, database performance, and database security and privacy. He has published numerous papers in conferences such as SIGMOD, VLDB, ICDE, and EDBT, and journals such as TODS, TKDE, and VLDBJ. Kian-Lee is a member of ACM. Kian-Lee is a co-Editor-in-Chief of the VLDB Journal, an Associate Editor of the IEEE Transactions on Knowledge and Data Engineering and WWW Journal. He was the Technical program co-chair of VLDB'2010, and ICDE'2011.

Printed in the United States
by Baker & Taylor Publisher Services